CYBER
LAW

With thanks to my editor, Debra Stollenwerk, for giving me the opportunity to write this book and for her assistance, guidance, and encouragement, all of which made this book better.

With love, admiration, and appreciation for my husband Bryan and my daughters Maureen and Aliza. You all helped me in ways too numerous to mention. Thank you for your patience, understanding, support, and, above all, your love.

CYBER LAW

Maximizing Safety and Minimizing Risk in Classrooms

Aimée M. Bissonette, J.D.

CORWIN
A SAGE Company

Copyright © 2009 by Aimée M. Bissonette

For information:

Corwin
A SAGE Company
2455 Teller Road
Thousand Oaks, California 91320
(800) 233-9936
Fax: (800) 417-2466
www.corwinpress.com

SAGE Ltd.
1 Oliver's Yard
55 City Road
London EC1Y 1SP
United Kingdom

SAGE Pvt. Ltd.
B 1/I 1 Mohan Cooperative
Industrial Area
Mathura Road,
New Delhi 110 044
India

SAGE Asia-Pacific Pte. Ltd.
33 Pekin Street #02-01
Far East Square
Singapore 048763

Printed in the United States of America

Library of Congress Cataloging-in-Publication Data

Bissonette, Aimée M.
Cyber law : maximizing safety and minimizing risk in classrooms / Aimée M. Bissonette.
  p. cm.
Includes bibliographical references and index.
ISBN 978-1-4129-6614-6 (cloth : alk. paper)
ISBN 978-1-4129-6615-3 (pbk. : alk. paper)
  1. Computer-assisted instruction—Law and legislation--United States.
2. Educational technology—Law and legislation--United States. 3. Internet—Law and legislation—United States. 4. Bullying in schools—Automation.
5. Cyberbullying. I. Title. II. Title: Maximizing safety and minimizing risk in classrooms.

KF4209.E38B57 2009
343.7309'944—dc22   2008054110

This book is printed on acid-free paper.

09   10   11   12   13   10   9   8   7   6   5   4   3   2   1

Acquisitions Editor: Debra Stollenwerk
Associate Editor: Julie McNall
Production Editor: Veronica Stapleton
Copy Editor: Codi Bowman
Typesetter: C&M Digitals (P) Ltd.
Proofreader: Dennis W. Webb
Indexer: Sheila Bodell
Cover Designer: Karine Hovsepian

Contents

Acknowledgments

I would like to thank the Edina Public Schools, Edina, Minnesota, for allowing use of portions of its Internet Acceptable Use and Safety Policy (Policy 524) as sample policy language in various chapters. Thanks also to Dr. Karen Sorvaag, Dr. Scott McLeod, Dr. Michael Burke, and John Arikian for their valuable input during the book's development.

Corwin and the author would like to thank the following individuals for their assistance.

Marla Davenport
Director of Learning and Technology
Technology and Information Education Services
St. Paul, MN

Lisa Graham, NBCT
Program Specialist, Special Education
Curriculum & Staff Development
Vallejo City Unified School District
Vallejo, CA

Carol S. Holzberg, PhD
Technology Coordinator
Greenfield Public Schools
Greenfield, MA

Cheryl Oakes
Collaborative Content Coach for Technology
Wells Ogunquit Community School District
Wells, ME

Dr. Stephen Zsiray
Consultant
Logan, UT

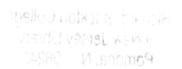

About the Author

Aimée M. Bissonette, J.D., is a lawyer, teacher, and writer. She has written extensively for trade publications and conducts training sessions for corporate, educational, and nonprofit groups (nationally and internationally) on the topics of copyright, rights negotiation and licensing, and the legal issues associated with technology in the schools. She has written Web site copy for two Web sites on intellectual property and copyright law and has written and coproduced a satellite broadcast for the Minnesota State Colleges and Universities titled *Copyright Considerations for Higher Education.* She practices law with Little Buffalo Law & Consulting in Minneapolis, Minnesota.

Introduction

Legal regulation of education is not new. It has just become a lot more complicated now that computers are in the classroom. The 21st-century classroom is markedly different from classrooms of the past. In the 21st-century classroom, teachers deliver computer-assisted and Web-based lessons; students conduct **Internet** research, accessing sources from across the globe; departments develop curriculum based on course content supplied by major universities; and students engage in real-time communication with scientists and explorers conducting experiments and traversing polar regions. The 21st-century classroom is not without pitfalls. It is well stocked with nonschool resources—iPods, cell phones, digital cameras, and recording devices—found in the hands, pockets, and backpacks of its students. These devices come with their own set of educational and legal problems. Lawmakers are trying to keep up, but the reality is, that is not always possible. As a result, the job of managing the day-to-day legal issues relating to technology falls squarely on schools.

This book is intended to help schools manage those legal issues. It is written for those on the "front lines": the teacher in the classroom, the librarian in the media center, and the information technology (IT) staff person monitoring Internet access, many of whom are *digital immigrants* still working to learn and adapt to the technology that their students, the *digital natives*, have been exposed to since birth. It is also written for the school administrator charged with drafting and enforcing school policy, particularly policy that relates to the growing array of electronic devices available to students, teachers, and staff in our kindergarten through Grade 12 schools.

With these readers in mind, this book has three main goals. First, the book is intended to provide some context for the application of civil and criminal laws in the K–12 classroom where computers and the Internet are used. This is provided primarily through the introductory scenarios at the beginning of the chapters and the legal discussion of the scenarios that follows.

Second, it is intended that readers of this book will experience a heightened awareness of the legal implications and risks of technology in the classroom and will be encouraged to develop preventative strategies— the proverbial ounce of prevention. Material to support this is provided in the discussion of laws and how these laws apply to schools, as well as the sections in each chapter that focus on the role of the schools.

Third, the book is intended to provide its readers with practical first steps, information that will allow schools to take action. This is accomplished by the addition of special features to this book: the sample policy language, the sidebars citing to helpful resources, and the end of chapter checklists and resource lists that help readers gauge where their schools stand on the legal issues discussed.

HOW THIS BOOK IS ORGANIZED

With the exception of the final chapter, each chapter begins with three scenarios based on actual occurrences in K–12 schools. The scenarios are followed by an analysis of the current law. The K–12 school's role in or response to the issues is then examined and supplemented by a discussion of strategies schools have successfully employed. Sidebars and sample policies are included, with helpful links to resources. In addition, checklists are included at the end of each chapter that assist readers in evaluating their schools' position with regard to the issues presented and to help identify strategies schools may adopt to more effectively position themselves to deal with **liability** risks.

HOW TO USE THIS BOOK

Keep the different sources of law in mind as you read this book. (See Resource A: How Laws Affect the Schools and Teachers Who Embrace Technology in Learning for a discussion of the different sources of law.) Where **statutory laws** are involved, ask whether your school's policies and procedures comply with the law as written. Where **common law** cases are discussed, ask yourself whether similar cases could arise in your school district and what action could be taken by your school district to reduce the risk of lawsuits. And finally, where school policy is reviewed, consider which options might work for your school district or whether other options exist that are not discussed in this book. Keep the flexible nature of **contract law** in mind, and be creative in crafting the best *law* for your school.

The ever changing technological terrain demands flexibility and smarts. Schools that work to understand technology, brainstorm options, tap available resources, and create action plans will be well ahead of the curve. Those schools will be able to capitalize on all the benefits technology brings to the educational environment. Just as important, they will reduce the risks of legal distractions and legal actions for their students, teachers, parents, and communities.

DISCLAIMER

The information in this book is not legal advice and is not intended as legal advice. It is intended to provide general legal information. It does not cover all issues related to the topics discussed. The specific facts that apply to your matter may make the outcome different than you might anticipate based on the material presented in this book. Please consult with your own attorney in regard to specific issues.

CHAPTER ONE

Cyberbullying

Curbing Student Use of Technology
to Intimidate and Harass Others

A 13-year-old Vermont boy was bullied for months online. Fellow students sent the boy a steady stream of instant messages calling him gay, taunting him, and insulting him. The boy sunk into depression and, ultimately, committed suicide. At the urging of the boy's father, state legislators proposed a law mandating that all Vermont schools adopt and implement comprehensive policies addressing cyberbullying.

A high-school student allowed her boyfriend to photograph her in the nude in a sexually suggestive position. Their relationship eventually ended, at which time the boyfriend posted the photograph on the Internet for all of their classmates to see. The student was inundated with sexual offers and threats.

Several athletes were secretly videotaped with hidden cameras in locker rooms, showers, and bathrooms. The videotaped images were sold to companies that posted them on the Internet. The athletes sued school officials in federal court, claiming the officials failed to detect the cameras and prevent the videotaping.

For as long as there have been schools, there have been bullies. Students know it. Teachers know it too. There are physical bullies, verbal bullies, and relational bullies (i.e., bullies who use their status to exclude others from social groups and activities). Bullies are aggressive and intimidating, and their behavior can have a devastating effect on their victims, both at school and at home.

Bullying poses a problem for schools because of the toll it takes on members of the school community and the school environment in general. As a result, many schools have enacted antibullying policies that allow them to take disciplinary action against bullies when bullies are caught in the act of harassing, taunting, or harming their peers. As the scenarios above indicate, bullying has changed markedly with the development of electronic media. In the case of the Vermont teen, it even prompted lawmakers to propose a law requiring school antibullying policies. This new form of bullying is called **cyberbullying.**

CYBERBULLYING

Cyberbullying differs from traditional, face-to-face bullying. It relies on electronic devices, the Internet, and the anonymity the Internet provides. Nearly all cyberbullies operate anonymously, hiding behind screen names or stolen identities. They can access their victims at any hour of the day, and they can reach much larger audiences electronically when spreading rumors and falsehoods.

Cyberbullies have a multitude of tools available to them: cell phones, camera phones, e-mail, instant messaging, personal Web sites, **social-networking sites,** and more. They bully their victims via text messages, postings on social-networking sites like Facebook and MySpace (or the more vitriolic Snubster, EnemyBook, Juicy Campus, and HateBook), and discussions in online chat rooms. They forward e-mail messages to huge groups of friends and post embarrassing, sometimes altered, photographs and video clips of their victims to the Internet. In some instances, students hack into other students' e-mail accounts or social-networking sites and create havoc by sending hateful messages or posting inflammatory content that appears to have been authored by their victims. The victims are not always fellow students. Sometimes the victims are teachers.

Common Forms of Cyberbullying

- *Flaming* is online fights using electronic messages with angry and vulgar language.
- *Harassment* is repeatedly sending nasty, mean, and insulting messages.
- *Denigration* is dissing someone online, sending or posting gossip or rumors about a person to damage his or her reputation or friendships.
- *Impersonation* is pretending to be someone else and sending or posting material to get that person in trouble or danger or damage that person's reputation or friendships.
- *Outing* is sharing someone's secrets or embarrassing information or images online.
- *Trickery* is tricking someone into revealing secrets or embarrassing information, then sharing it online.

(Continued)

(Continued)

- *Exclusion* is intentionally and cruelly excluding someone from an online group.
- *Cyberstalking* is repeated, intense harassment and denigration that includes threats or creates significant fear.

Source: Willard, N. (2005). An educator's guide to cyberbullying and cyberthreats: Responding to the challenge of online social aggression, threats, and distress. *Center for Safe and Responsible Use of the Internet.* http://csriu.org/cyberbully/docs/cbcteducator.pdf

What do studies tell us about cyberbullies and their victims? Interestingly, females are more likely to be cyberbullies than males. In all likelihood, this is because cyberbullies, unlike traditional bullies, don't need to be physically superior to their victims. Cyberbullies rely on verbal, emotional, and psychological attacks, like those inflicted on the Vermont teen described above.

Another characteristic of cyberbullies is that they thrive on the anonymity technology provides. Cyberbullies can assume any name, any persona, any gender they want and, in doing so, often can disguise the source of the bullying. In 2006, for example, a Missouri teen named Megan committed suicide when someone who had befriended her online suddenly turned on her and sent increasingly hostile and degrading messages. The online friend identified himself as a 16-year-old boy named Josh and exchanged messages with Megan for several weeks before he started bullying her. An investigation after Megan's death revealed that Josh did not exist. He was the online persona of the mother of another teenage girl with whom Megan had been fighting.

What else is typical of cyberbullies? Cyberbullies are likely to act without first thinking through the consequences of their action. The second scenario above may be an example of this. The boyfriend probably wanted to embarrass his former girlfriend, but he may not have anticipated or intended the level of embarrassment and shame he caused her when he posted her photograph online. The impulsivity of cyberbullies is directly related to the tools available to them. Those tools allow them instant access to their victims and a wide audience for their bullying behavior. As was stated by Darby Dickerson (2005) in the article *Cyberbullies on Campus,* "Technology allows bullies to be meaner, more frequently, with more allies, before an inestimable audience."

THE LAW AND CYBERBULLYING

Technology is developing at a rapid pace, and the law is struggling to catch up. The number and variety of digital devices, along with easy access to the Internet, have resulted in a range of scenarios lawmakers never anticipated. Legislators are scrambling to enact laws, but it is not always clear what those laws should say or govern. The available case law on **free speech,** defamation, sexual harassment, and assault cannot easily be applied to cases of cyberbullying, and the rulings by courts around the country are inconsistent. Where the law and cyberbullying are concerned, one thing is certain, though. Parents of bullied students are taking action. They are seeking protection and compensation from the courts, and their lawsuits frequently name schools as defendants.

As Tresa Baldas points out in her article *As 'Cyber-Bullying' Grows, So Do Lawsuits,* schools are "in a legal quandary: If they punish a student for something they did off school grounds, they could get hit with a freedom of speech claim. If they do nothing, they could get hit with failure to act litigation."

There is no question that schools can and should intervene when cyberbullying occurs on school grounds or via the school's computer system. But what if the cyberbullying occurs outside of school? In keeping with earlier free speech decisions, courts generally evaluate a school's right to intervene in off-campus bullying by determining whether the cyberbullying *harmed* the victim's educational experience or *disrupted* the classroom. Harm might be demonstrated by a showing that the victim was unable to concentrate at school, suffered a measurable drop in grades, or had an increasing number of absences that coincided with an escalation in the bullying. Disruption to the classroom might be demonstrated by fights or arguments between students at school, the origins of which can be traced to the cyberbullying. Without a finding of harm or disruption, courts generally rule in favor of the bully on free speech grounds.

Legislators at the state and municipal levels have tried to tackle the cyberbullying problem as well. Several states have enacted legislation requiring public schools to draft and enforce antibullying policies that specifically address cyberbullying, and a great number more are considering enacting the same or similar legislation. These laws may provide important support for schools that take disciplinary action against students engaged in off-campus bullying.

The Missouri municipality where Megan lived has criminalized cyberbullying. It passed its anticyberbullying law in direct response to the cyberbullying incident that led to her suicide. As described above, the bully in that instance was not another student but the mother of a student who posed online as a 16-year-old boy named Josh. Residents of the town, outraged by the mother's actions and the apparent inability of state prosecutors to hold her criminally liable for her actions, pushed for the law that now makes cyberbullying a misdemeanor crime, punishable by a fine of up to $500 and 90 days in jail, regardless of whether the bullying is school related or not.

State and federal prosecutors are becoming more aggressive and more creative in pursuing cyberbullies too. In 2008, the mother in Megan's case was indicted by a federal grand jury and charged with one count of conspiracy and three counts of accessing protected computers without authorization to get information used to inflict emotional distress. It was the first time the federal **statute** on accessing protected computers was used in a cyberbullying case. The mother pled not guilty and moved to have the charges dismissed. A ruling on her motion was still pending when this book went to print.

In Texas and Wisconsin cases similar to the second example above (the example in which the teen posted nude pictures of his former girlfriend), prosecutors have brought charges of child pornography, sexual exploitation of a child, and defamation against teens who have posted nude photos of other students to MySpace pages or forwarded the photos via cell phone to other students.

THE ROLE OF THE SCHOOLS

As the scenarios indicate, cyberbullies have access to their victims in school (e.g., when a student sends intimidating text messages to another student in class or uses a cell phone camera to capture a locker room scene) and outside of school (e.g., when students make disparaging remarks about other students or their teachers on their MySpace pages). In both instances, cyberbullying can make victims fear for their safety and can impact their ability to learn if victims are so inundated with bullying messages that they are more focused on avoiding the bullies than on their coursework.

The negative effect of cyberbullying on bystanders should not be overlooked either. In fact, many experts assert that the role of bystanders (what they should and should not do) should be a key focus of all cyberbullying-prevention programs.

Schools that fail to take action to curb cyberbullying among students may find themselves defending their actions (or lack of action) in court or, worse still, dealing with the tragedy of a student suicide. As is indicated above (and as is explained in greater detail in the next chapter), schools have not yet been held legally liable for cyberbullying by students using nonschool computer resources, outside of school hours and off school premises, because schools have little control over that behavior and intervening raises student free speech concerns. The legal landscape is changing, though, particularly as legislators across the country propose legal solutions to the bullying problem, many of which involve action by schools.

POLICY

What can schools do to curb cyberbullying? Obviously, schools need to examine their existing antibullying policies and amend them, as necessary, to include prohibitions against cyberbullying. In drafting cyberbullying additions to their policies, schools should note that experts warn against highly punitive policies. **Zero-tolerance policies** are not recommended. Among other things, the punishments that result from such policies (e.g., suspension or expulsion) may be so severe as to actually discourage children and adults from reporting the cyberbullying they observe. Parents who know their child is the target of another student's mean-spirited text messages may want school authorities to intervene to try to stop the text messaging, but may hold off on reporting the conduct to the school if the school's only option for intervening is suspending the student. Policies that allow for a range of sanctions from verbal warnings, to detention, to suspension or expulsion and that equate the appropriate sanctions with the actual cyberbullying conduct are more likely to encourage early and more frequent reports of cyberbullying that school authorities can nip in the bud.

What are the other attributes of a good cyberbullying policy? Good policies contain good definitions. Cyberbullying must be defined in such a way that students, parents, and staff clearly understand what the term encompasses. In those states in which there are laws mandating antibullying policies, it may be helpful to describe bullying in precisely the same language as is used in the statute. Policies should include references to intimidation, teasing, threatening, and defaming behavior and specifically mention the

---

Tips for On-the-Spot Bullying Intervention:

- Immediately stop the bullying.
- Refer to the bullying behavior and to the relevant school rules against bullying.
- Support the bullied child in a way that allows him or her to regain self-control, to "save face," and to feel supported and safe from retaliation.
- Include bystanders in the conversation and give them guidance about how they might appropriately intervene or get help next time.
- If appropriate, impose immediate consequences for students who bully others.
- Do not require the students to meet and work things out.
- Provide follow-up interventions, as needed, for the students who were bullied and for those who bullied.
- Notify parents of children who are involved, as appropriate.

Source: The U.S. Department of Health and Human Services www.stopbullyingnow.hrsa.gov.

cyberbully's tools of the trade: e-mail, text messages, instant messages, digital images, blogs, and social-networking sites.

The breadth of the policy should also be noted. Policies should expressly state that they apply to all instances of cyberbullying, whether on or off campus, with or without the use of school resources. Although such a statement does not dispense with student free speech claims entirely, it helps to provide a basis or rationale for school action in cases where off-campus cyberbullying interferes with the school's mission or impacts the safety and welfare of members of the school community.

Policies should also describe the procedures victims, witnesses, and bystanders use to report cyberbullying, including whether teachers and staff are mandatory reporters and the steps the school will take to investigate those reports. (Many schools develop and distribute easy-to-use bullying report forms for use by students and staff.) If there are different reporting procedures for parents, the policy should outline those as well.

Policies should detail how and when parents will be notified of cyberbullying incidents. For instance, whether parents will be alerted of a first instance or only after a pattern of cyberbullying has been established, and whether the school will alert only the parents of the victim or the parents of the victim and the bully. If the school intends to gather data relating to bullying incidents, the policy should also outline how data will be collected and whether and when such data will be made available to the public.

Last, schools should consider drafting specific policies relating to cell phones, cameras, handheld scanners, and other electronic communications devices. Specific policies aimed at particularly prevalent or problematic student behavior can help keep bullying in check on campus. For example, restricting student use of camera phones and other recording devices may help avert incidents like the one described in the third scenario above where athletes were the victims of unauthorized filming.

Student Use of Electronic Communications Devices: Sample Policies

Restrictive Policy

Students shall not possess or use an electronic communications device while on school property (or while attending a school-sponsored activity on or off school property). An "electronic communications device" is a device that emits an audible signal, vibrates, displays a message, or otherwise summons or delivers a communication to the possessor.

A student, at the request of his or her parent and with permission of the school principal, may possess an electronic communications device if for health or extraordinary reasons. Use of the device must be in accordance with the agreement between the requesting parent and the school principal.

A person who discovers a student in possession of an electronic communications device in violation of this policy will report the violation to the principal.

Middle-Ground Policy

Students may possess and use cellular telephones, pagers, or other electronic communications devices, subject to limitations of this and other policies of the district. Parental permission is required. Use of the device shall be limited to the period before classes begin in the morning, during the student's lunch period, and after the student's last class in the afternoon. Such devices shall not be used during instructional time or in the passing time between classes unless during an emergency.

Building principals may promulgate rules to enforce this policy at the building level.

Students violating the policy may be subject to disciplinary action.

Liberal Policy

Students shall be allowed to use and possess electronic communications devices on school property. The superintendent or building principal shall deal with any abuses of the privilege afforded under this policy at the building level under current disciplinary policies concerning disruption of the educational environment.

EDUCATION

Well-crafted policy is important, but it alone will not remedy the cyberbullying problem. As Shariff and Johnny (2007) point out in their article *Cyber-Libel and Cyber-Bullying: Can Schools Protect Student Reputations and Free-Expression in Virtual Environments?*, policy alone "does not teach students to think about the impact of their actions; nor does it engage them in dialogue about how they can address the challenges that new technologies bring, in an informed, thoughtful and coherent manner." Schools need to supplement cyberbullying policies with educational efforts aimed at all members of the school community.

A number of nonprofit groups and government agencies have compiled materials on the topic of bullying, including posters, tip sheets, book marks, and interactive Web sites that engage students in problem-solving scenarios about bullying. These materials are available at low or no cost to schools.

The U.S. Department of Health and Human Services also provides a wide range of materials for school students, staff, teachers, and parents in downloadable PDF form on its Web site www.stopbullyingnow.hrsa.gov. Among other things, the site advocates that schools engage in an initial investigatory period before launching antibullying campaigns to assess the level of bullying in their schools. The site recommends that schools survey students, teachers, and staff about the nature, extent, and location of bullying in their schools; talk with staff members about their perceptions of bullying and their current efforts to address bullying; and hold an open house or community meeting to solicit parent feedback about bullying and bullying prevention needs at school.

School efforts to reduce cyberbullying should include staff development training for teachers, staff, and administrators about cyberbullying, its effects, and how to intervene. Adults who witness cyberbullying often want to intervene to stop the bullying behavior, but they may not know the best way to do so. Schools need to provide support and training to all the adults who come into contact with students, including bus drivers, cafeteria workers, custodians, and school nurses.

Finally, a commitment to educating students about high-tech courtesies is essential to a successful antibullying effort. Schools are ideally situated to teach students about the proper use of technology and the consequences of misuse. They can incorporate discussions about the ethical use of the Internet and other electronic media into classroom instruction and into the larger school environment via posters and public service announcements. They also can make an effort to identify and reward students who demonstrate positive, inclusive behavior.

CONCLUSION

Cyberbullies are in our schools, and the tools available to these bullies likely will multiply over time. Left unchecked, today's student bullies will become tomorrow's bullying neighbors, coworkers, and bosses. But schools are not without recourse. Schools do not have to tolerate cyberbullying. They can adopt and enforce policies to clearly signal that bullying is not acceptable and will be punished. Just as important, schools can lead the way in educating technology users about responsible and respectful use of electronic media.

DEALING WITH CYBERBULLIES
TIPS FOR KIDS

▶ **Ignore the person.** Sometimes the easiest thing to do is to ignore the person and go on about your business. Log-off if the harassment is bothering you.

▶ **Block or delete the person.** If it is happening on Instant Messaging or some other place online that requires a "buddy list," you can block certain users based upon their username, or delete them if they are in your buddy list. You can also block e-mails that are being received from specific e-mail addresses.

▶ **Change your information.** If someone has hacked into your profile, change your password. If someone repeatedly sends you messages (like, "add me to your buddy list" over and over), consider changing your username or e-mail address.

▶ **If there is a profile that was created about you without your knowledge,** contact the company which runs the site to have the profile or language taken off.

▶ **If you are upset about what is being said, talk to someone you trust.** Don't feel like you're alone. Many times, you are able to take care of the cyberbullying on your own. Sometimes, it gets out of hand though, and it's helpful to talk to an adult about what is going on. If you feel scared or overwhelmed, maybe even trapped, it's definitely time to talk to an adult, inform your Internet Service Provider and possibly call the police if you are getting physical threats.

For more information, go to
www.cyberbully411.org

DEALING WITH CYBERBULLIES
TIPS FOR KIDS

▶ **Never** arrange to meet with someone you met online unless your parents, friends, or a trusted adult go with you. If you are meeting them, make sure it is in a public place.

▶ For additional information on this topic:

▶ Visit **www.cyberbully411.org**

▶ Visit **www.GetNetWise.org**

▶ Visit your library

▶ The NetSafe Bookmarks are available as print-ready PDF files at:

▶ **www.ila.org/netsafe**

SAFE BLOGGING
TIPS FOR TEENS

▶ **Be anonymous.** Avoid postings that could help a stranger to locate you. This includes your last name, address, phone numbers, sports teams, the town you live in, and where you hang out.

▶ **Protect your info.** Check to see if your service has a "friends" list that allows you to decide who can visit your profile or blog. If so, allow only people you know and trust.

▶ **Avoid in-person meetings.** Don't get together with someone you "meet" in a profile or blog unless you are certain of their actual identity. Talk it over with an adult first. Although it's still not risk-free, arrange any meetings in a public place and bring along some friends, your parents, or a trusted adult.

▶ **Think before you post.** What's uploaded to the Net can be downloaded by anyone and passed around or posted online pretty much forever. Avoid posting photos that allow people to identify you, especially sexually suggestive images.

SPONSORED BY
ILLINOIS LIBRARY ASSOCIATION · ILA · myspace.com a place for friends
ALA American Library Association

SAFE BLOGGING
TIPS FOR TEENS

▶ **Check comments regularly.** Don't respond to mean or embarrassing comments.

▶ **Be honest about your age.** Membership rules are there to protect people. If you are too young to sign up, don't lie about your age.

▶ For additional information on this topic:

　▶ Visit **www.ConnectSafely.org**

　▶ Visit **www.GetNetWise.org**

　▶ Visit your library

▶ The NetSafe Bookmarks are available as print-ready PDF files at:

　▶ **www.ila.org/netsafe**

SPONSORED BY
ILLINOIS LIBRARY ASSOCIATION · ILA · myspace.com a place for friends
ALA American Library Association

SOCIAL NETWORKING
TIPS FOR PARENTS

▶ **Be reasonable and try to set reasonable expectations.** Pulling the plug on your child's Internet activities is rarely a good first response to a problem—it's too easy for them to "go underground" and establish accounts at a friend's house or many other places.

▶ **Be open with your children.** Encourage them to come to you if they encounter a problem online—cultivate trust and communication because no rules, laws or filtering software can replace you as their first line of defense.

▶ **Talk with your children.** Find out how they use the services. Make sure they understand basic Internet safety guidelines, including privacy protection and passwords, the risks involved in posting personal information, avoiding in-person meetings, and not posting inappropriate photos.

▶ **Consider requiring that all online activity take place in a central area of the home, not in a child's bedroom.** Be aware that there are also ways children can access the Internet away from home.

SOCIAL NETWORKING
TIPS FOR PARENTS

▶ **Try to get your children to share their blogs or online profiles with you.** Be aware that they can have multiple accounts on multiple services. Use search engines and the search tools on social-networking sites to search for your child's identifying information.

▶ For additional information on this topic:

▶ Visit **www.ConnectSafely.org**

▶ Visit **www.GetNetWise.org**

▶ Visit your library

▶ The NetSafe Bookmarks are available as print-ready PDF files at:
▶ **www.ila.org/netsafe**

A series of NetSafe bookmarks developed by the Illinois Library Association in conjunction with MySpace.com and the American Library Association. The bookmarks provide tips on three important topics: dealing with cyberbullies, safe blogging for teens, and social-networking tips for parents. They can be purchased at a nominal cost but also are available as free, print-ready PDF files at http://www.ila.org/netsafe.

Checklist for Reducing Cyberbullying

Has your district done the following?

☐ **Addressed cyberbullying directly?** School district policies that do not specifically mention cyberbullying do not provide sufficient protection to students or schools. Define cyberbullying and state that it will not be tolerated. Be clear about the punishment that can result from violations of the cyberbullying policy.

☐ **Established cyberbullying complaint procedures?** Establish a confidential reporting system. Ensure that all complaints, whether from students, parents, or staff, are acknowledged and investigated promptly.

☐ **Educated its teachers and staff about cyberbullying?** Provide professional development or inservice opportunities for teachers and staff (including bus drivers, school nurses, and cafeteria workers) to inform them about cyberbullying and help them to more readily spot bullying behavior among students.

☐ **Designed and implemented a districtwide campaign against cyberbullying?** Invite a guest speaker to a school board or PTO meeting. Incorporate antibullying public service messages into morning announcements or school assemblies. A number of nonprofit agencies have cyberbullying materials (e.g., posters, bookmarks, and Web-based, interactive instructional guides) available for free or at low cost to schools. Obtain and distribute these in school and at special events.

☐ **Involved parents in cyberbullying discussions?** Host an open house for parents and solicit parent feedback about student Internet use and cyberbullying. Provide parents with tip sheets and resources to help them identify and respond to cyberbullying.

☐ **Included sections on cyberbullying in its Internet education curriculum?** For examples of age appropriate approaches to cyber-bullying go to http://www.cyberbully411.org and http://www.netsmartz.org/resources/reallife.htm for older kids and www.mcgruff.org for younger kids.

☐ **Provided protection for students who are victims of cyber-bullying?** Create a buddy system or other support mechanism for the bullied student. Offer the services of school counselors or mental health professionals to victims and bullies alike.

Online Resources

Center for Safe and Responsible Internet Use.

http://www.cyberbully.org/cyberbully/

Cyberbullying.us.

http://cyberbullying.us/index.php

McLeod, S. (2006). *Can schools regulate cyberbullying, harassment, and social networking?*

http://www.slideshare.net/mcleod/can-schools-regulate-cyberbullying harassment-and-social-networking

Stop Cyberbullying.

http://www.stopcyberbullying.org/index2.html

CHAPTER TWO

Student Use of the Internet

Reducing Inappropriate Internet Behaviors

A group of high-school students secretly recorded their teacher in the classroom, and later, uploaded the video to YouTube with audio commentary on the teacher's alleged lack of hygiene and poor organizational skills. The video included footage of the teacher walking away from the camera and bending over, accompanied by the rap song "Ms. New Booty." Several students were suspended for their roles in creating and posting the video, one of whom filed a lawsuit in federal court challenging his suspension on free speech grounds.

An unidentified person (presumed to be a student) recorded a teacher as she attended an outdoor fifth-grade graduation ceremony, filming the teacher's face, down the length of her body, then zooming in on her bottom. The video was posted to YouTube accompanied by the Van Halen song "Hot for Teacher." The teacher was made aware of the video, complained to YouTube, and the video ultimately was taken down, but not before being viewed 200,000 times. The video then resurfaced on the social-networking site MySpace.

More than one hundred high-school students at a Minnesota school were disciplined for violating "no alcohol" pledges they had made in conjunction with their participation in athletics and other extracurricular activities when Facebook photos of the students drinking alcohol were brought to the attention of school officials. The students did not deny the authenticity of the photos, but claimed that the disciplinary actions against them were inappropriate because the school had violated their rights by reviewing and responding to their private photos.

These examples describe actual Internet conduct by students. Some of them involve legally actionable conduct; others involve ethical miscues. The key question with regard to all of them, though, is whether they involve legally protected speech. U.S. citizens enjoy a constitutionally protected right to free speech and that right extends to students. As a result, it is not always easy to tell when schools may take disciplinary action against students for inappropriate e-mail and Internet expression. Often, student expression, no matter how offensive, falls into the category of legally protected speech. This means schools must tread lightly or risk a lawsuit themselves.

If student e-mail and Internet expressions are not deemed to be legally protected speech, a number of legal claims can be asserted against the student and, in some cases, the school. These claims include libel, slander, harassment, invasion of privacy, and negligence. In most instances, these claims will be brought by the person who is identified in or is the target of the e-mail or Internet expressions against the student who posted the harmful information. If school computers or the school's Internet system were used, or if teachers or staff were aware of the postings, schools might be named in these lawsuits as well. In those instances, the schools would be accused of negligence for their failure to monitor student use of school computers or failure to intervene when they became aware there was a problem.

As the above examples illustrate, inappropriate student speech can have a devastating effect on the classroom, the lives of students and teachers, and the school's overall ability to carry out its educational mission. Accordingly, schools must teach students appropriate use of e-mail, the Internet, and the multitude of other electronic devices available to today's students.

FREE SPEECH

As is stated above, there are many legal claims that can arise as a result of student misuse of the Internet. These claims arise when students post false, highly private, or otherwise harmful information about others to the Internet, whether in personal blogs, on social-networking sites such as Facebook, in e-mails, or in text messages. In one recent incident, for example, a group of unnamed Indianapolis high-school students created a fake Facebook profile for a high-school dean and sent out inappropriate messages and images presumably from the dean to students. The outraged dean filed a lawsuit alleging harassment and identity theft, citing damage to his reputation. Thereafter, the judge in the matter ordered Facebook to provide Internet providers (IPs) and other identifying information so the identities of the students could be determined and the students held accountable.

Individuals, like the dean described above, whose reputations have been damaged base their claims on the same legal standards whether the harmful speech is conveyed electronically, in print, or orally. In cases where the speech is conveyed electronically, however, the money awarded to successful plaintiffs often is much higher. Offensive speech posted on the Internet has the likelihood of reaching many more people than non-electronic speech and, thus, can cause significantly greater harm.

There are instances, however, when students' inappropriate, even offensive use of the Internet must be tolerated. Students have the right to comment on and criticize their teachers, their schools, fellow students, and other members of the school community. In many instances, information posted on the Internet by students, though rude or hurtful, is considered protected free speech under the **First Amendment** to the U.S. Constitution. The postings may be unethical or in poor taste, but they are not legally actionable.

The First Amendment to the U.S. Constitution states as follows: "Congress shall make no law respecting an establishment of religion, or prohibiting the free exercise thereof; or abridging the freedom of speech, or of the press; or the right of the people peaceable to assemble, and to petition the government for a redress of grievances." This language has been interpreted by our courts on numerous occasions.

In cases involving students, U.S. courts have affirmed that students are entitled to free expression within certain limits. The problem, of course, is that many of these cases were decided preInternet, and the limits outlined by the courts in these preInternet cases are not easily applied to cases involving today's technology.

Overview of Key U.S. Supreme Court Decisions on Student Free Speech

Four U.S. Supreme Court cases set standards for students' freedom of expression in cyberspace.

In *Tinker v. Des Moines Independent Community School District*, 393 U.S. 503 (1969), three students were suspended from school for wearing black armbands to protest the Vietnam War. In ruling that the suspensions violated the students' free speech rights, the Court held that students have a right to free speech in school settings unless the speech materially disrupts a school's ability to carry out its mission in an orderly fashion or unless the speech infringes upon the rights of others to be free from harassment.

In *Bethel School District 403 v. Fraser*, 478 U.S. 675 (1986), the Court held that schools may prohibit speech that undermines their basic educational mission. In this case, Matthew Fraser gave a student government campaign speech at a student assembly that contained sexual innuendo. In upholding

Fraser's suspension, the Court emphasized that schools need to maintain control over student behavior and also noted that schools have a role in teaching students the "appropriate form of civil discourse" and preparing students for participation in a democratic society.

In *Hazelwood School District v. Kuhlmeier,* 484 U.S. 260 (1988), a principal removed several articles from the school newspaper. The Court supported the principal's actions, stating the student newspaper was not a public forum and was not intended for unrestricted use by the students. The Court ruled that schools could exercise greater control over activities that might be considered part of school curricula or were conducted under school sponsorship and that student speech restrictions could include not only speech that would "substantially interfere with [a school's] work" but also speech that is, for example, poorly written, ungrammatical, inadequately researched, biased or prejudiced, vulgar or profane, or unsuitable for immature audiences. In response to *Hazelwood,* several states enacted Anti-Hazelwood laws, granting student journalists greater free speech protections.

In *Morse v. Frederick,* 551 U.S. ___, 127 S. Ct. 2618 (U.S. 2007), a student refused to take down a sign reading BONG HiTS 4 JESUS at an off-campus, school-sanctioned activity. Principal Morse confiscated the banner and later suspended the student because his banner appeared to advocate illegal drug use in violation of school policy. The Court held that because schools may take steps to safeguard those entrusted to their care from speech that can reasonably be regarded as encouraging illegal drug use, the school officials in this case did not violate the student's First Amendment free speech rights.

Case law clearly states that schools may reasonably restrict the speech of students on campus. However, a lot of student Internet activity takes place off campus. Case law also states that schools may take action when the content of student speech constitutes a material disruption to class work or involves substantial disorder or invasion of the rights of others. A great deal of student Internet speech does not rise to this level, though. Accordingly, courts confronted with today's cases involving blogs, social-networking sites, **YouTube** postings, and the like face a tremendous challenge. They need to craft legal opinions that fit within the boundaries of existing U.S. case law but fully account for our ever expanding electronic school environment.

On-Campus Activity

Under existing case law, one of the important factors in determining when and whether schools may restrict student speech is location

---
Sample Policy Language: Declaring the School System a Limited Forum

The school district's computer network is considered a limited forum; therefore, the district may restrict speech for valid educational reasons. Uses which might be acceptable on a user's private personal account on another system may not be acceptable on this limited-purpose network.

Source: Internet Acceptable Use and Safety Policy (Policy 524), Edina Public Schools.

(i.e., whether the speech takes place on campus or off campus). Because schools provide, maintain, and pay for school Internet systems, they generally may limit student use of such systems. Legally speaking, a school may place reasonable restrictions on the speech of students using the school Internet system by declaring the system a **limited forum.** This means the school may restrict obscene, profane, rude, and discriminatory speech, criminal or dangerous speech, speech that could cause damage or that presents a danger for the school or members of the school community, and speech that abuses or clogs the school Internet system (e.g., spam). The first example above illustrates this well.

In the first example, students recorded a teacher in her classroom during school hours and without her permission. The teacher wasn't aware she was being filmed but others in the classroom were. Moreover, the filming took place while the teacher was actively involved in instruction. The students involved in the recording filmed each other clowning around and even stood behind the teacher at one point making faces and rabbit ears over her head.

When the YouTube posting was discovered, the students were suspended. At least one of the students challenged the suspensions arguing that the posting of the video on the Internet was protected free speech. The school stood by its decision to suspend the students, however, citing its right to place reasonable restrictions on student on-campus speech. The school asserted that the students violated a school policy prohibiting recording devices in class and, in addition, that the filming of the teacher caused a material disruption to class work, one of the few exceptions to student free speech.

Incidents in two Texas schools provide additional examples of appropriate school action with regard to disruptive student speech. In the first, a school district confiscated dozens of student cell phones upon learning that nude images of two junior-high-school girls were being circulated among members of the student body. The girls took the photos themselves and sent them to their boyfriends via cell phone. The boyfriends forwarded the photos to friends who, in turn, forwarded them on to others in the school. In the second incident, five eighth-grade students were suspended after one of them took a cell phone photo of a 13-year-old girl coming out of the shower and circulated it. Similar incidents have been reported in Alabama, Colorado, Connecticut, New Jersey, New York, Pennsylvania, and Utah.

Although some questioned the authority of the schools in these instances to confiscate phones and suspend students, at least one legal scholar stated support for the schools' actions. Adam Gershowitz, a professor of law at South Texas College of Law, commented that actions of this type likely fall within a school district's authority, particularly because the pictures being circulated were of under-age children. The circulation of the photos took place on campus, and the material disruption to class work was apparent. Both schools also had policies relating to cell phone use in school. Students are entitled to free speech, but not when their speech impinges on the school's educational endeavors.

Off-Campus Activity

Student off-campus speech is not as easily addressed by schools. If the students in the first example had filmed the teacher outside the classroom while she was not engaged in teaching, their speech (posting the video to YouTube) likely would have been protected. Students have the right to criticize their teachers, whether by uploading video to YouTube, posting comments to RateMyTeachers.com, or in general conversation. The second example above illustrates this point.

The second example depicts protected student speech, despite the negative impact of the speech (the posted video) on the teacher involved, because there was no obvious violation of school policy and no material disruption to class work. The video, although suggestive and embarrassing, did not defame the teacher and did not violate her privacy rights. The teacher in this example had little recourse. Even if she had been successful in determining who recorded and posted the video, she would not have been able to take legal action because the video provides insufficient grounds for a claim of defamation, invasion of privacy, or other civil lawsuit. The law governing free speech generally allows this type of public recording. The subsequent posting of the video in this example falls within free speech parameters as well.

What if the off-campus speech is highly critical or aimed at specific individuals associated with the school? May schools take action then?

Schools walk a tightrope when challenging this type of student speech and are cautioned against acting in haste. In Oceanport, New Jersey, a school district was sued by the parents of an eighth-grade student, when the school punished the student for posting material that was critical of the school on a Web site that he maintained on his own time from his own home computer. The student's Web site had a guest book on which visitors could post comments about the Web site or the school. The student voluntarily included a statement on the guest book, though, that no posting should contain profanity or threats. When school officials learned of the Web site, they suspended the student for a week, banned him from playing on the baseball team for a month, refused to allow him to go on a class field trip, refused to allow him to take the placement tests for two honors classes, and did not announce his award for a high SAT score when similar student awards were announced. The U.S. District Court ruled in favor of the student, finding that the school presented no evidence that the student's own comments were either threatening or created a substantial disruption. The school district ended up paying the student $117,500 to settle his free speech claim. (See *Dwyer v. Oceanport School District, et al.*, No. 03–6005 D. N.J. filed March 31, 2005) (granting student summary judgment on liability issues).

A high-school student in a seemingly similar case did not enjoy the same success as the New Jersey eighth grader, however, when she sued her school district on free speech grounds. In that case, a school principal barred the high-school senior from running for and then serving as senior class secretary (the principal would not allow the student's name to be put on the ballot, but the student won the election as a result of write-in votes), and speaking at her graduation because of derogatory and allegedly false statements she made about school officials in a blog. A U.S. district court judge ruled against the student when she requested an injunction, and the student appealed.

The Second Circuit Court of Appeals wrestled with the same questions as the court in *Dwyer*, yet came to a very different conclusion. The Second Circuit held that it was reasonably foreseeable that the high-school student's postings on her publicly accessible blog (in which she referred to school administrators as "douche bags" and encouraged other students to call and e-mail the school superintendent to "piss her off") would create a risk of substantial disruption within the school environment. (See *Doninger v. Niehoff*, No. 07–3885 2nd Cir. May 29, 2008).

In explaining its decision, the Second Circuit cited *Tinker* (see the sidebar, Overview of Key US Supreme Court Decisions on Student Free Speech). It also stated that "it is of no small significance that the discipline here related to [the high school student's] extracurricular role as a student government leader," and that "participation in voluntary, extracurricular activities is a 'privilege' that can be rescinded." As of the time of this writing, the U.S. Supreme Court had yet to rule on this issue of the scope of a school's authority to regulate student speech that does not occur on school grounds or at a school-sponsored event. Whether and to what extent the Second Circuit's decision on this issue of student off-campus speech will be applied by other courts remains to be seen, but the ruling has caused a stir.

There is one type of student speech schools still seem to be able to respond to without fear of legal repercussions: speech involving threats or references to violence. When threats or references to violence are involved, schools may take action, even if the speech takes place off campus and outside of school hours. The law is clear that student speech is not protected when it involves substantial disorder or invasion of the rights of others. Threats and references to violence clearly fall within this exception. For example, school authorities rightfully took action when a teenage boy who was angry about a grade he received posted a video to YouTube identifying his math teacher and asking viewers to "shoot her in the neck." The teen was suspended from school, taken into custody, and charged with aggravated assault. Members of the school community who learn of such threats need to contact school officials immediately.

The third example above differs from the first two in that the issue is not whether the information posted to the Internet by students was protected, but whether school officials acted appropriately in viewing Internet postings and disciplining students. The example describes an incident at a Minnesota high school, but similar incidents have occurred at other schools across the country. These incidents highlight the fact that students often do not understand that what they post to the Internet is not private. The students in the Minnesota example believed that school officials violated their right of privacy by viewing photographs posted on personal Web sites, despite knowing that hundreds of people had access to their sites.

THE SCHOOL'S ROLE

Schools need to draft and enforce school policies regarding appropriate conduct on campus. In fact, such policies are critical for schools that do not want to be held liable for inappropriate use of the school Internet system. In drafting these policies, schools need to anticipate the many ways in which students might use or misuse the school's Internet system. For instance, many schools draft policies that prohibit on-campus use of recording devices by students, except where the recording is associated with a class assignment or other approved school activity. The school in the first example at the beginning of this chapter had such a policy in place, which is one reason it was successful in taking action against the students involved.

Educating students about appropriate off-campus Internet conduct is also the domain of the schools. As is stated above, schools are not *legally* required to monitor the off-campus Internet speech of their students unless schools are made aware of threats or references to violence. That does not mean that schools should ignore off-campus use of computers and the Internet, though. Schools make computers and the Internet available in the classroom and provide guidelines for their school related use. Shouldn't educating students about the appropriate use of these tools extend beyond the classroom?

Sample Policy Language: Possible Repercussions for Student Off-Campus Internet Activity:

A student or employee engaging in [unacceptable uses] of the Internet when off school district premises and without the use of the school district system also may be in violation of this policy as well as other school district policies. In situations when the school district receives a report of an unacceptable use originating from a nonschool computer or resource, the school district may investigate such reports to the best of its ability. Students or employees may be subject to academic sanctions or disciplinary action for such conduct including, but not limited to, suspension or cancellation of the use or access to the school district computer system and the Internet and discipline under other appropriate school district policies, including suspension, expulsion, exclusion, or termination of employment.

Source: Internet Acceptable Use and Safety Policy (Policy 524), Edina Public Schools.

Schools are ideally situated to advise students about the repercussions of Internet postings, the need to limit the amount of information posted on Web sites and blogs, and the long-term effects of such postings. The students involved in the third example suffered some minor disciplinary measures (e.g., temporary suspension from school athletic teams), but the consequences could have been far greater. Potential employers and college admissions officers conduct their own Internet searches now. The type of behavior depicted in the photos posted by the students in the example above could easily result in the loss of a job opportunity or rejection of an application for admission to a desired college.

Schools can work to appropriately channel student speech, too. Some schools offer students an opportunity to provide feedback to school administrators about teachers, classes, and the school in general through a confidential, but respectful, complaint process. Providing students with an opportunity to be heard while providing guidance with regard to how best to raise issues with school officials helps students develop lifelong tools for conflict resolution and encourages ethical behavior.

CONCLUSION

Schools need to help students understand the long-term effect of today's blogging, postings, and practical jokes. Talking to students and educating them about appropriate Internet conduct not only will help prevent student free speech disputes and potential school liability but will help students become better Internet citizens. It does not matter if the speech involved takes place in a student newspaper or on MySpace or YouTube, or is communicated through some other medium yet to be invented, the lessons are the same. Schools are ideally positioned to help students learn how to make the most of their free speech rights.

Checklist for Curbing Inappropriate Internet Behavior of Students

Has your district done the following?

☐ **Drafted school policies regarding appropriate use of school Internet resources?** Under the Communications Decency Act, schools that have a written policy regarding appropriate use of school Internet systems are provided immunity from liability for misuse of Internet resources where the school has no control or supervisory responsibilities related to the student use of the system. Schools without such a policy do not enjoy immunity.

☐ **Drafted policies governing on-campus use of recording devices and cell phones?** Schools should institute written rules governing on-campus use of recording devices or cell phones. Many districts choose to prohibit use of such devices except where the recording is associated with a class assignment or other approved school activity.

☐ **Instructed students about appropriate off-campus Internet and social-networking conduct?** By educating students with regard to appropriate Internet and social-networking conduct, student misuse of these technologies in a manner that impacts schools might be minimized or avoided. Students may also benefit with regard to employment and higher education opportunities if they are better aware of the risks and hazards of inappropriate use.

(Continued)

(Continued)

☐ **Designed mechanisms to constructively channel student speech?** By offering students an opportunity to provide confidential, constructive feedback to administrators about teachers, classes, and other school related issues, schools may reduce misuse of technology resources and aid students in developing conflict resolution skills.

Online Resources

Lesson Plan: Understand your Acceptable Use Policy. *CyberSmart!* *http://www.cybersmartcurriculum.org/*

Strategies for Schools in the Age of the Social Web. *bNetS@vvy* http://bnetsavvy .org/wp/test-post-for-social-networking/

CHAPTER THREE

Staff Use
of the Internet

*Drawing a Line Between
Teachers' Public and Private Lives*

A school superintendent in Illinois was suspended by the school board for making inappropriate use of videotaped interviews of new teachers. The superintendent spliced his own gag questions into the interviews to spoof the new faculty members, making it appear that they were killers, strippers, and drug users. He aired the video during a back-to-school staff seminar and posted it on the district's Web site.

Virginia public school officials fired a high-school art teacher after learning via a YouTube video that the teacher moonlighted by creating paintings using his bare buttocks and other body parts. In the video, the teacher wore a swim thong and a mask while demonstrating how he applies paint to his body and presses it onto the canvas. The teacher used a pseudonym in the video. He also used the pseudonym on the Web site he created to display and sell his art. In response to the firing, the teacher filed a lawsuit against the school board, a school district personnel official, and the principal of the high school, alleging a violation of his free speech rights.

An openly gay substitute teacher was removed from the substitute-teacher call list in an Ohio school district after reports surfaced that he made reference to a middle-school student's sexuality and included detailed accounts of his interactions with other students on his personal Web site. The teacher did not mention students or the schools at which he had worked by name, but his Web site included explicit musings about sexual acts and photographs of the teacher in his underwear. The Ohio Department of Education has a policy that permits investigations of teachers accused of conduct unbecoming the teaching profession.

The first two chapters of this book discuss student misuse of the Internet. As the above examples illustrate, however, misuse of the Internet is not restricted to students. Teachers and staff also engage in questionable Internet activity. As with students, some of that activity raises questions of free speech, and some of it is legally actionable.

A review of legal cases dealing with teacher free speech, including what teachers may discuss in the classroom and what they publicly may say during their hours off, reveals that courts are issuing inconsistent and, in some cases, irreconcilable decisions. The wide-ranging decisions and the ambiguity those decisions have created put school districts at risk and leave teachers with little guidance as to what they may and may not say personally and professionally. At a minimum, it appears that because of their position and status within the greater community, K–12 teachers and staffs have not been treated leniently by the courts where free speech is concerned. Teacher associations and legal counsel for school districts are warning teachers to be careful about what they post online.

Overview of Key U.S. Supreme Court Decisions on Teacher Free Speech

Two leading U.S. Supreme Court cases set standards for teachers' free speech rights in school settings.

In *Pickering v. Board of Education,* 391 U.S. 563 (1968), a teacher wrote a letter to a local newspaper criticizing the school board regarding school funding issues. The school board fired the teacher, claiming the letter contained false statements and damaged the reputations of board members and school administrators. The Court overturned the firing, ruling that teachers as public employees may not constitutionally be compelled to give up First Amendment rights they would otherwise enjoy as citizens. The court established a balancing test under which the interests of a school board as an employer must be weighed against the interests of a teacher as a citizen.

However, in *Connick v. Myers,* 461 U.S. 138 (1983), the Court upheld the firing of an assistant district attorney who, in response to an unwanted change of duties, prepared a questionnaire soliciting fellow staff members' opinions on office transfer policies, morale, need for grievance procedures, and whether employees felt pressure to work in political campaigns. The Court upheld the termination, emphasizing that the speech in question must address "a matter of public concern" for First Amendment protection to arise. After *Connick,* many courts have found teacher speech to relate to matters of private rather than public concern.

The free speech rights of public school teachers and staff hinge on a number of factors including whether the speech occurred in the classroom or off duty, whether the speech was conveyed via the school's Internet system, whether the speech involved a protected topic (e.g., unionizing, employment conditions, or whistle blowing), and whether the speech disrupted the workplace. The right of schools to restrict the on-campus speech of public school teachers has long been recognized, even in instances where the necessity of restricting the speech might be questioned. As an example, in August of 2008, an elementary school principal in Minnesota was suspended and ultimately fired for conduct unbecoming a teacher when he sent flirtatious e-mails on the school Internet system to a teacher with whom he had a consensual relationship.

What about the off-campus speech of teachers? Right or wrong, recent trends seem to indicate that the off-campus speech of public school teachers is also being scrutinized and to a much greater extent than that of the average individual. School policies have been expanded in some instances to apply to teacher Internet activity outside of the classroom, blurring the line between teachers' public and private lives.

As is the case with student Internet speech, the legal gray area for teacher free speech is off-campus activity. Although reasonable restrictions may be placed on teachers and staff using school Internet systems, the same may not be true when teachers and staff post material to personal Web sites, blogs, or social-networking sites not associated with the school's Internet system. The World Wide Web is a **public forum,** and the courts are split as to how much control schools have over teachers and staff who use their own computers and Internet systems to express their views. The First Amendment entitles public employees to express their concerns about matters of public interest, and as the above examples indicate, other expressions may be legally protected as well.

The first example above is of obvious legal concern. It also points out that adults can harbor the same basic misconceptions about the Internet as students. There is no indication that the school superintendent in the first example intended any harm; in fact, it appeared that he thought his actions were comical. Had he restricted his airing of the videotape to the back-to-school staff seminar, the matter may have been nothing more than an example of poor judgment. However, when the superintendent took the additional step of posting the video on the district's Web site his actions could no longer be easily excused because what was so obviously a spoof to him was made available for viewing by members of the school community and others far beyond the geographic boundaries of the school community. The potential harm to the reputations of the teachers he spoofed was greatly enlarged when he posted the video to the Web site, as was his exposure to legal claims. The disruption to the workplace caused by his posting of the video overrode any free speech claims the superintendent may have had.

By contrast, the second example above involves a teacher who took pains to separate his professional life as a public school teacher from his personal life as an artist. This example is a great illustration of the tension between a teacher's role as a very public member of the community and his right as an individual to free expression. It raises the question of how far schools can go in monitoring the off-duty behavior of teachers. Was it appropriate, in this instance, for the school to terminate the teacher for off-duty behavior it deemed questionable when the teacher attempted to conceal his identity as a public school teacher and was engaging in legal activity? Robert Ashmore and Brian Herman discuss the difficulty of this issue in their 2006 article, "Abuse in Cyberspace," pointing out that failing to recognize teachers' free speech rights can result in legal liability for schools, but that "administrators also must be prepared to identify unprotected speech and determine when Internet postings are causing material disruptions or resulting in a flow of inappropriate materials into the school."

The third example above raises the issue of greatest concern. This example does not merely relate to the off-duty Internet activity of a teacher, it raises concerns about student privacy, an issue which is analyzed in detail in Chapter 4. Although the teacher in this example did not identify students by name, he may have provided sufficient information for those students to be identified. This example also illustrates the overlap between state and federal law. Teachers, like all of us, have certain entitlements under the First Amendment of the U.S. Constitution; however, teachers also are governed by state licensing laws. Failure to comply with licensing laws can result in the suspension of a teacher's license. Here the teacher's conduct in describing students on his personal Web site not only raised an issue as to whether his speech was disruptive and therefore not protected but also brought his professional integrity into question. Schools may investigate and react to off-duty speech that affects school functioning and student safety.

Another highly publicized free speech case involving off-campus Internet speech concerned a student teacher who was denied a teaching degree the day before her college graduation because of material she had posted online. Twenty-seven-year old Stacy Snyder, an undergraduate at Millersville University, was denied a teaching degree despite having completed all of her required course work because of a photo she posted of herself on a personal Web site, a MySpace page. The photo was from a 2005 Halloween party and showed Ms. Snyder wearing a pirate hat and holding a plastic cup. Beneath the photo, Ms. Snyder had placed the caption "Drunken Pirate."

Ms. Snyder posted the photo on her MySpace page using her own computer and Internet system; however, it was brought to the attention of the officials of Conestoga Valley High School, the school at which Ms. Snyder was a student teacher. As a result of the posting, and because Ms. Snyder reportedly had demonstrated problems with respect to her class-room competence and "over-familiarity" with students, Conestoga Valley gave Ms. Snyder a rating of "unsatisfactory" on the professionalism por-tion of her student teacher evaluation.

Days before Ms. Snyder's graduation, Millersville University informed her that it would not award her a teaching degree, but would be awarding her a degree in English instead. Unable to work as a teacher, Ms. Snyder took a job as a nanny and sued Millersville in federal court, claiming, among other things, that Millersville violated her free speech rights. A judge ultimately ruled against her, finding that her role as a student teacher was akin to that of a public employee and, accordingly, that her speech (i.e. the posted photo) was not entitled to First Amendment protection because it did not involve a matter of public con-cern. *Snyder v. Millersville University, et al,* No. 07-1660 (Dec. 3, 2008, E.D. Pa).

Ms. Snyder's case and the second scenario above highlight the dilemma facing schools today. Even if a school administrator thinks a teacher's personal Website is inappropriate, offensive, or damaging to the school's reputation, free speech protections may apply. It is risky for schools to take action without fully weighing the legal consequences. Conestoga Valley and Millersville's responses ultimately passed legal muster, but only after lengthy litigation. The school district in the second example above avoided litigation by settling the art teacher's wrongful termination suit out of court.

THE SCHOOL'S ROLE

Many of the problems associated with teacher and staff misuse of the Internet can be avoided through communication. School administra-tors, teachers, and staff need to discuss appropriate on-campus Internet activity, as well as the expectations each has with regard to the other where off-duty communications are involved. Obviously, schools need clear, well-written policies relating to the use of school computers, e-mails, and the school Internet system. They need to take the additional step, though, of ensuring that teachers and staff under-stand these policies.

Schools need to draft and enforce policies relating to teacher and staff Internet use that inform teachers and staff about important concerns in the school community relating to privacy and personal safety of members of the school community. Policies can also be used to alert teachers and

Sample Policy Language

Communications of Public School Employees Subject to Data Practices Acts

School employees should be aware that data and other materials in files maintained on the school district system may be subject to review, disclosure, or discovery under [the State Data Practices Act].

Source: Internet Acceptable Use and Safety Policy (Policy 524), Edina Public Schools

staff to the fact that the electronic communications of public school employees can be accessed under public records laws, something that may not be generally known.

As is mentioned above and in the previous chapter, school policies should declare school Internet systems limited forum systems that may be used for noncommercial, educational purposes only. By describing school Internet systems in this way, schools achieve a measure of control over what otherwise might be considered a public forum for free speech purposes.

Schools may also draft policies regarding off-campus speech. These policies advise teachers and staff about how and whether the school will monitor off-campus speech. For example, several Mississippi schools concerned about communications between students and teachers crossing the line between professional and personal have enacted or are considering policies that prohibit online communication on social-networking sites or via text messaging between students and teachers. Off-campus speech policies also include employee blogging policies and policies that prescribe rules for all teacher-authored personal Web pages.

Sample Internet Social-Networking and Blogging Policy

In general, the school respects the right of employees to participate in social-networking sites (e.g., MySpace, Facebook), personal Web sites, and Weblogs, away from work. It respects the right of employees to use them as a medium of self-expression. However, because readers of such social-networking sites, Weblogs, or personal Web sites may view the employee as a representative or spokesperson of the school, the school requires, as a condition of employment, that employees observe the following guidelines when referring to the school, its students, programs, activities, volunteers, or other employees:

1. Employees must be respectful in all communications related to or referencing (by word, photo, or other means) the school, its students, programs, activities, volunteers, or other employees.

2. Employees must not use obscenities, profanity, or vulgar language.

3. Employees must not use social-networking sites, Weblogs, or personal Web sites to disparage the school, its students, programs, activities, volunteers, or other employees.

4. Employees must not use social-networking sites, Weblogs, or personal Web sites to harass, bully, or intimidate the school's students, volunteers, or other employees. Behaviors that constitute harassment and bullying include, but are not limited to, comments that are derogatory, with respect to race, religion, gender, sexual orientation, color, or disability; sexually suggestive, humiliating, or demeaning comments; and threats to stalk, haze, or physically injure a student, volunteer, or other employee.

5. Employees must not use social-networking sites, Weblogs, or personal Web sites to display, or discuss engaging in, conduct that is prohibited by school policies or professional codes of ethics, including, but not limited to, the use of alcohol and drugs, sexual behavior, sexual harassment, and bullying.

6. Employees must not post photos of school activities, students, volunteers, or other employees on the employee's social-networking site, Weblog, or personal Web sites without obtaining written permission. In the case of students, even where written permission is given, employees must adhere to the rules stated in the school's privacy policy with regard to identifying students.

7. Employees must not post photos of themselves, students, volunteers, or other employees while wearing school uniforms, or other identifiers that link those pictured to the school.

8. The use of the school name or logo is not allowed without written permission.

9. Linking or referencing an employee's social-networking site, Weblog, or personal Web site to the school's Web site is not allowed without written permission.

Any employee found to be in violation of any portion of this Internet Social-networking and Blogging Policy will be subject to immediate disciplinary action, up to and including termination of employment.

   In addition, the school reserves the right to publicly access an employee's social-networking site, Weblog, or personal Web site as part of its decision-making process with respect to promotions and other human relations management requirements and considerations. Where applicable, employees may be asked to provide access as part of an employment selection and/or promotion process.

Source: YMCA, Kingston, Ontario.

It is important to note, however, that policies do not always have to be restrictive. In response to the increasing number of questions brought before it concerning what teachers can and cannot say in public about school district policies, personnel issues, and school operations, the Charleston County, South Carolina school board created an employee free speech policy. The Charleston school board opted to create a specific policy affirming its teachers' right to speak their minds about events occurring in the school district without fear of being penalized, harassed, or disciplined in any way.

Whether all schools should follow the Charleston example is a matter for discussion, of course, but the Charleston school board's message arguably is a good one: Schools need to communicate to their teachers and staff when and how schools will react to complaints about off-campus activity and, ideally, that schools support the right of teachers and staff to speak out on matters of public concern, even when those matters reflect poorly on the school.

CONCLUSION

The law regarding teacher and staff on-campus speech is pretty clear. Schools may restrict classroom speech and speech that utilizes school computers and the school's Internet system.

The law regarding off-campus speech is less clear. Schools are encouraged to discuss off-campus speech with teachers and to memorialize decisions regarding when and how they will monitor the off-campus speech of teachers and staff in policies. Decisions regarding off-campus speech should be made only after considering the effect of monitoring such speech on morale, the expenditure of school resources necessary for monitoring, and the potential legal repercussions as gauged by school legal counsel. At the very least, however, the matter should be broached directly with teachers and staff. Training teachers and staff on appropriate Internet use is just as important in the school setting as the equivalent training for students.

Checklist for Addressing Teacher and Staff Use of the Internet

Has your district done the following?

☐ **Drafted a well-written policy relating to the use of school computers, e-mails, and the school Internet system?** School administrators, teachers, and staff need to establish clear rules and expectations for appropriate on-campus Internet use.

❏ **Defined the school Internet system as a limited forum system?** By limiting use of school Internet systems to noncommercial, educational purposes only, schools may achieve a greater measure of control over what otherwise might be considered a public forum for free speech purposes.

❏ **Drafted policies regarding off-campus speech of teachers and staff?** Schools should inform administrators, teachers, and staff about how and whether the school will monitor off-campus speech. Well-articulated blogging and social-networking policies and Web page requirements for teacher-authored Web pages help protect teachers, students, and districts from liability for potential Internet misuse and disclosure of private student information.

Online Resources

ACLU. *Free Speech Rights of Public School Teachers.*

http://www.aclu-wa.org/detail.cfm?id=59

Edutopia. The George Lucas Educational Foundation.

http://www.edutopia.org/

International Society for Technology in Education (ISTE). *Educator Resources.*

http://www.iste.org/AM/Template.cfm?Section=Educator_Resources

Linder, D. *Free Speech Rights of Public Employees.*

http://www.law.umkc.edu/faculty/projects/ftrials/conlaw/publicemployees.htm

PBS Teachers. *Professional Development for PreK–12 Educators.*

http://www.pbs.org/teacherline/

Testing Whether the Government Has Violated First Amendment Rights of Employees.

http://www.law.umkc.edu/faculty/projects/ftrials/conlaw/employpunishment.html

CHAPTER FOUR

Privacy and Security

Protecting Student Information

A growing number of school districts are purchasing thumbprint scanners and other **biometric identification tools** for use by students when paying for meals, logging their attendance, boarding buses, and checking out library books. Use of these tools has eliminated the need for lunch money or library cards. Parents, however, are not entirely persuaded that the time- and money-saving advantages biometric tools offer outweigh the risks of collecting and storing this type of student information. Some states have passed laws requiring schools to obtain parental permission before scanning student fingerprints. Other states have banned the use of biometrics in schools entirely.

A computer malfunction wiped out a month's worth of grades at three high schools and one middle school in Indiana, two weeks before report cards were to be issued. Some of the district's teachers had printed hard copies of their grade reports but most had not. The district was unable to recover the data, much to the dismay of high-performing students and to the joy of students who had not been performing well and who were given a fresh start when the grade information could not be recovered.

A high-school football coach overheard a conversation in the locker room that made him think two of his star players were struggling in the classroom and might be placed on academic probation. If the players were placed on probation, they would not be allowed to play the final games of the season, including play-offs. The next day, when the coach sees one of the school counselors in the faculty lounge, the coach asks the counselor if there is any way she can verify the information he heard about the players. Later that day, the counselor leaves a voice mail for the coach, assuring him that both players are okay grade-wise, but just barely. She encourages the coach to talk to the players about taking advantage of the school's math tutoring lab.

As the above scenarios indicate, there are a number of ways student information can be obtained, stored, and accessed. Schools have always kept records on students, but more and more, those records are being kept in electronic form. This raises a number of privacy concerns. Parents and students are concerned about how schools are storing student information and what student information is being posted on school Web sites and in electronic grade books. Parents and students are also concerned about the sharing of student information among teachers and staff members or with others outside the school community. Another area of concern involves student self-disclosure of private information. Inappropriate storage and posting of information, breaches of confidentiality among staff, and self-disclosure by students pose tremendous risks to students and schools.

PRIVACY LAW

The key piece of legislation relating to student privacy is the **Family Educational Rights and Privacy Act (FERPA) of 1974,** 20 U.S.C. §1232g; 34 CFR Part 99. FERPA affects the use, storage, and dissemination of student education records. FERPA has implications for schools that store and transmit student records electronically or post student photographs and work on school Web sites.

FERPA requires parental notice and consent before schools can post or otherwise disclose private student information. As the first scenario above indicates, parents are highly concerned about the disclosure of student information. Even the gathering of private information with no intent to disclose, as in the case of the thumbprint scanners, can cause concern. In such instances, parental consent may not be required under the law, but failure to communicate with parents about the proposed gathering of information may produce an outcry and put the school in the position of having to defend a legitimate action.

RECORDS STORAGE AND RETENTION

FERPA also affects a school's storage and retention of student records. Because students and parents are allowed to inspect and review student educational records, schools need to provide adequate mechanisms to store and retain those records. The second example above illustrates the risk associated with inadequate storage of records.

Family Educational Rights and Privacy Act (FERPA)

Generally, schools must have written permission from the parent or eligible student to release any information from a student's education record. However, FERPA allows schools to disclose those records, without consent, to the following parties under the following conditions:

- School officials with legitimate educational interest
- Other schools to which a student is transferring
- Specified officials for audit or evaluation purposes
- Appropriate parties in connection with financial aid to a student
- Organizations conducting certain studies for or on behalf of the school
- Accrediting organizations
- To comply with a judicial order or lawfully issued subpoena
- Appropriate officials in cases of health and safety emergencies
- State and local authorities, within a juvenile justice system, pursuant to specific state law.

From U.S. Department of Education at http://www.ed.gov/policy/gen/guid/fpco/ferpa/index.html.

Storing records as electronic records only and having an inadequate backup mechanism is risky. In the example involving the lost grade records, the school indicated that the effect on students was minimal because students only lost a few weeks' worth of grades. To the student who performed particularly well during those few weeks, though, the loss of the data is significant. As a result of the data loss, students who had performed well were placed on the same level as students who had performed poorly. What if the loss had covered more than a few weeks or affected the grades of high-school seniors applying to college? The school's failure to provide adequate backup for its records in that instance could have affected its students' opportunities with regard to college admission and scholarships.

Failure to adequately store and retain records also can lead to problems for schools involved in litigation. A 2006 amendment to the Federal Rules of Civil Procedure provides that evidence stored in personal computers, PDAs, printers, cell phones, and digital voicemail may be accessed and used in lawsuits. This means, among other things, that schools must make relevant student records available when school-related litigation arises. If a school is involved in a lawsuit and is unable to retrieve relevant student records, the school could be sanctioned by the court, and the court could effectively rule against the school by allowing certain legal presumptions against the school.

INFORMATION SHARING AMONG STAFF

Teachers and staff generally are aware of their legal responsibilities relating to the sharing of confidential student information with individuals outside the school community. When it comes to sharing information with teachers or staff members within the school community, however, whether intentionally or inadvertently, that awareness seems to decrease. As the third scenario above illustrates, many teachers and staff mistakenly believe they may share confidential student information, including grades, with other teachers or staff members within the school. This is not the case. Casual information sharing among teachers and staff is problematic in and of itself, but there are additional implications when information is shared electronically, especially when it is shared with people who legally have no right to it.

The third example above describes an incident of intentional and illegal information sharing. The football coach has no legal right to the student's grade information. The counselor has no legal right to share it. In other instances, information sharing may be inadvertent but can be just as damaging. It can result, for example, when teachers share passwords and create an opportunity for others to access student personal records. Inadvertent sharing can also occur when teachers fail to use password-protected screen savers, leave information displayed on their computer screens when they are not at their desks or in their rooms, or leave printed information on shared printers. Teachers and staff need to be educated about the potential risks involved in not treating confidential information with care and not keeping it out of the reach of prying eyes.

STUDENT SELF-DISCLOSURE

The third area of concern with regard to privacy is student self-disclosure. Although some personal disclosure is to be expected and, in fact, may be appropriate (e.g., the high school student writing an article for an online student newspaper or filling out an online request for materials from a college), many students exceed the bounds of what is safe by disclosing personal information, including contact information, online. As was stated previously, rules regarding student self-disclosure of confidential information, at least with regard to student use of school computers and the school Internet system, are often enumerated in school Internet policies. But what about student disclosure of information on social-networking sites or commercial Web sites?

Student disclosure of information is a tremendous area of concern. Commercial Web sites frequently solicit personal information from students through surveys, contests, and games, and then use the information to engage in targeted marketing. Many commercial Web sites lack privacy policies, and few have a mechanism for obtaining parental consent. Even those Web sites that do require parental consent generally only do so for children under the age of 13. In many cases, students are not even aware that information is being collected. Experts speculate that these seemingly innocent disclosures could lead to an increase in identity theft.

Identity theft is not the only concern, of course. Researchers of Internet behavior have concluded that student disclosure of information is most risky when combined with talking online to people about sex. Teens are naturally prone to explore their sexual selves. If they do this online, though, and talk to strangers about sex, it increases the likelihood of meeting a sexual predator online. Older students need to understand that online disclosure, combined with suggestive talk, dramatically increases the chance that a predator will attempt off-line contact.

A number of attempts have been made by state and federal legislators to manage the problem of student self-disclosure, but these attempts have fallen short of curing the problem. The Children's Online Privacy Protection Act (COPA) (1999), for instance, was enacted in an attempt to police Web sites directed to children, as well as general Web sites that knowingly collect personal information from children. COPA's intent was to regulate when and what information could be collected electronically from children, when verifiable parental consent had to be obtained, what needed to be contained in a Web site privacy notice, and more. One problem with COPA was that it only applied to the collection of personal information from children under the age of 13. Even assuming there was a good way of policing the ages of Web site users, a cutoff at age 13 meant most student Internet users were not protected. Another problem, from a protection standpoint, was that COPA did not apply to chat rooms, YouTube, or other interactive Web sites— the exact places where students are known to disclose personal information. The U.S. Court of Appeals for the Third Circuit declared the problematic law unconstitutional in 2008, and the US Supreme Court declined further review of the matter in January of 2009, confirming not only that effective legislation of this type is difficult to draft, but that legislation alone is not likely to curb excessive or risky disclosure by students.

THE SCHOOL'S ROLE

To effectively address privacy concerns, schools need to formulate plans with regard to all three privacy trouble spots: inappropriate disclosure of information by the school, information sharing among teachers and staff, and student self-disclosure. By and large, inappropriate disclosure of information by schools can be avoided by strict adherence to FERPA. Many schools handle their FERPA obligations by requesting parental consent at the beginning of the school year via a global consent form. Some of these schools also follow up with specific consent forms or photograph release forms as events arise. As part of this process, schools must determine how and under what circumstances students will be identified. Schools may request consent from parents to identify students by a student's initials, by first name and last initial, or by student's full name. In the case of photos or video postings, schools may request consent from parents to identify students by display of the photo or video with no identification, with class identification, with event identification, or with full identification. Dealing with multiple consent forms requires an organized approach.

Some schools have dealt with the permission issue via policy. By drafting policies relating to the disclosure of student information, schools avoid the logistical issues associated with tracking consent forms for various events and students. Policies can address the disclosure of student information in Web site postings, video yearbooks, and the like and, frequently, are drafted with the ages and abilities of the school's particular students in mind. Schools that follow this approach establish disclosure standards, and then give parents an opportunity to disallow disclosure of their child's personal information by opting out. This policy approach requires a balancing of the interests of students and the school and is considered particularly effective for high-school-aged students, many of whom are directly involved in producing student activity group Web sites, student newspapers, student yearbooks, and the like.

In an effort to guard against inappropriate or unlawful information sharing, schools can adopt a number of approaches. The first and most obvious approach involves educating teachers and staff about FERPA and other privacy legislation. With regard to inadvertent and unintentional information sharing, schools frequently enlist their information technology (IT) staffs. The IT staffs can assist teachers and staff by installing password-protected screen savers, adjusting monitors so

Characteristics of a Strong Password

Strong passwords

- consist of at least six characters (the more characters, the stronger the password);
- have characters that are a combination of letters, numbers, and symbols;
- are typically case-sensitive and contain letters in both uppercase and lowercase; and
- do not contain words that can be found in a dictionary or parts of the user's own name.

they are out of public view, advising teachers and staff about **strong passwords** (i.e., passwords that are difficult for both humans and computer programs to detect), setting up independent, secure servers for the storage of sensitive data, helping teachers and staff configure home computers so they meet workplace security requirements, and providing mechanisms for the secure destruction of private data that has reached the end of its lifecycle. Schools may also provide continuing education courses on such topics as how to send effective electronic communications that do not require transmission of student data, sending communications with only the minimum required data, removing names and other identifiers from communications whenever possible, and selecting the most secure media for sharing private data.

With regard to student self-disclosure, educating students about the risks of self-disclosure is a primary consideration for schools. The self-disclosure issue is complicated and education about self-disclosure should be designed to deliver developmentally appropriate messages. For young children, the message is simple: No personal information should be shared online without an adult's permission. For teens, the message should focus on the inappropriateness of romantic advances from adults, the power imbalance between teens and adults, and the criminal nature of the adult's actions.

There are a number of online tutorials and Web-based programs available to schools for teaching students about the risks of self-disclosure. One such program, CyberSmart, offers grade specific curricula and activities focused on identifying commercial messages online and protecting private information. The Web site iSAFE.org provides Internet safety programs too. In one iSAFE activity, students are asked to review a transcript from a chat room conversation and identify the chat participants who divulged too much private information.

Schools also are addressing student self-disclosure by offering school-based social-networking sites like Imbee.com and Whyville .net. At Imbee.com, a social-networking site for children ages 8 to 14, built-in privacy features include a requirement that parents submit credit card numbers online to vouch for their children's identities and the ability to limit student interaction to a specific population, such as a ball team or student group. Whyville.net requires its users to spend three days familiarizing themselves with its site. Users then must pass a "chat license" test that includes questions about privacy and Internet safety before they can interact with others on the site. School-based sites like these allow schools to teach students responsible Internet conduct and appropriate levels of self-disclosure in a relatively safe, controlled environment.

CyberSmart!®

Name ______________________________ Date ____________

Safety with Cyberpals

I wonder what CJ looks like.

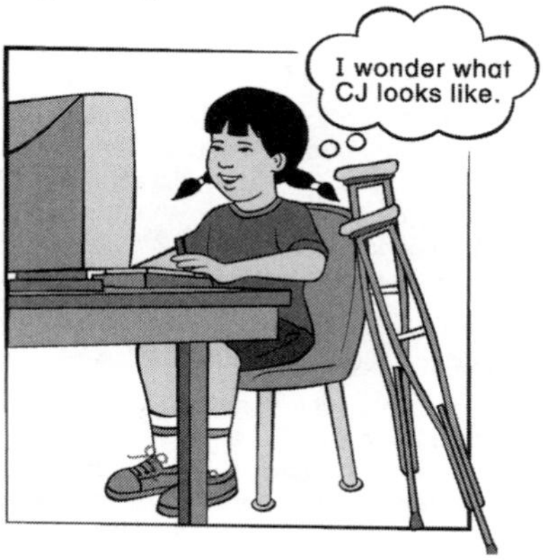

Sita likes to visit an online chat room where kids talk about school and homework. She really likes one of the people in the chat room, who uses the screen name "CJ." When Sita shares a problem she has at school, CJ gives good ideas for handling the problem. Other times CJ is a good listener. On many days, Sita and CJ plan what time they will chat the next day. Sita thinks of CJ as a close friend.

One day, while chatting, CJ and Sita compare their two schools. Sita types, "My school principal is so strict. We have to walk through the halls in straight lines!"

CJ answers, "My school isn't so strict. What's the name of your school?"

Sita types back, "Uh, my school's name is too hard to spell."

CJ types, "So, where is your school?"

What should Sita answer?

____

____

What makes this answer a good one?

____

____

____

Safety: ***Cyberpals***

Safety with Cyberpals
Activity Sheet 1 of 2

(Continued)

(Continued)

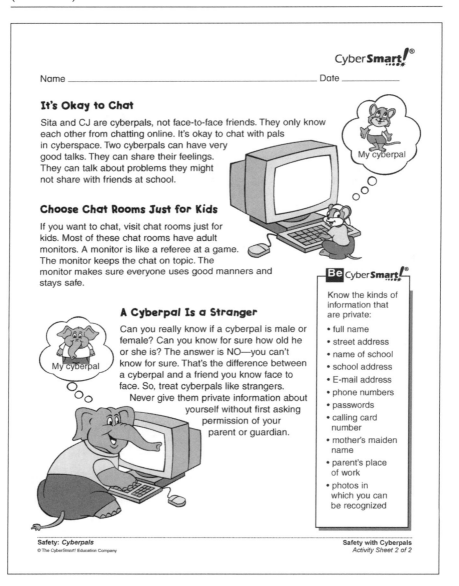

CyberSmart!®

Name _____   Date _____

It's Okay to Chat

Sita and CJ are cyberpals, not face-to-face friends. They only know each other from chatting online. It's okay to chat with pals in cyberspace. Two cyberpals can have very good talks. They can share their feelings. They can talk about problems they might not share with friends at school.

My cyberpal

Choose Chat Rooms Just for Kids

If you want to chat, visit chat rooms just for kids. Most of these chat rooms have adult monitors. A monitor is like a referee at a game. The monitor keeps the chat on topic. The monitor makes sure everyone uses good manners and stays safe.

A Cyberpal Is a Stranger

Can you really know if a cyberpal is male or female? Can you know for sure how old he or she is? The answer is NO—you can't know for sure. That's the difference between a cyberpal and a friend you know face to face. So, treat cyberpals like strangers. Never give them private information about yourself without first asking permission of your parent or guardian.

My cyberpal

Be CyberSmart!®

Know the kinds of information that are private:

- full name
- street address
- name of school
- school address
- E-mail address
- phone numbers
- passwords
- calling card number
- mother's maiden name
- parent's place of work
- photos in which you can be recognized

Safety: *Cyberpals*
© The CyberSmart! Education Company

Safety with Cyberpals
Activity Sheet 2 of 2

One in a series of age-specific lessons offered by CyberSmart! for use by schools.
http://www.cybersmartcurriculum.org/home/

CONCLUSION

Privacy concerns are not new to schools. Today's technology just makes it easier to access and share private information. Schools need to pay greater attention to how they store records, who has access to those records, and how those records are shared. Specific policies relating to electronically stored information must be drafted, and faculty and staff need to be educated about the liabilities associated with wrongful disclosure. In addition, schools need to educate students about the risks of online self-disclosure, both when using school computers and the school Internet system and when accessing the Internet off campus.

Checklist for Protecting Student Information

Has your district done the following?

☐ **Drafted well-written policies addressing the three privacy trouble spots?** Schools need well-articulated standards addressing disclosure of private information by the schools, sharing of information among teachers and staff, and for student self-disclosure of personal information.

☐ **Educated teachers and staff regarding FERPA and other privacy legislation?** Appropriate education and training may help avoid improper disclosure of private data by teachers and staff.

☐ **Enlisted legal counsel and IT staff to aid in protecting private data?** Installing password-protected screen savers, physically locating computer hardware in secure locations, setting up separate secure servers for storage of private data, and aiding teachers and staff in configuring home computers to meet workplace security requirements all help to protect private data. It is also important for schools to appropriately protect private data from inadvertent loss. Appropriate data retention policies and computer data back-up systems should be established.

☐ **Educated students about the risks of self-disclosure of private information?** Students are often unaware of the risks of disclosing private information online. A number of online tutorials and Web-based programs are available to train students to identify commercial messages online and protect personal data.

Online Resources

FERPA. 20 USC. § 1232g

    http://www4.law.cornell.edu/uscode/20/1232g.html

FERPA Regulations.

    http://www.ed.gov/policy/gen/reg/ferpa/index.html

Forum Guide to the Privacy of Student Information. (July 2006). National Forum on Education Statistics.

    http://nces.ed.gov/pubs2006/2006805.pdf

Protecting the Privacy of Student Records. (1997). National Center for Education Statistics and National Forum on Education Statistics.

    http://www.ed.gov/policy/gen/reg/ferpa/index.html

Protecting Student Privacy in Wisconsin.

    http://dpi.wi.gov/lbstat/dataprivacy.html

CHAPTER FIVE

The School as an Internet Service Provider

Providing Access and Protecting Students

A satellite provider discontinued service to the Navajo nation, leaving the entire reservation, including its schools and government, without Internet access. Service was discontinued as a result of a billing dispute in which $2.1 million of E-Rate funds were withheld by the federal government pending investigation of billing issues. Satellite service is the only option for the Navajo nation. Dial-up and wireless connections are not possible because of the lack of telephone service and a wireless grid on the reservation.

As part of a pilot program designed to increase opportunities for rural students, a school bus in Arkansas' rural Sheridan School District was outfitted with an Internet router. A group of students whose school commutes exceeded 15 hours per week were assigned to the bus and were provided with video iPods and laptops. The bus was stocked with educational videos. The goal of the project was to create a virtual one-room schoolhouse. The success of the program has spurred efforts to extend the program to other buses.

A high-school student using a school computer after school in the school library downloaded a sexually explicit image. Other students in the library saw the image but did not alert the librarian, who was working at her desk. One student told her parents about the incident. The parents called the principal the next morning, demanding that both the student who downloaded the image and the librarian be disciplined.

Although computer and Internet use is expanding exponentially in schools nationwide, there are still large numbers of students without access to technology. Not surprisingly, the underserved students are from the same groups that typically are deprived of high-end educational facilities and teachers. Included among this underserved population are racial minorities, the disabled, English language learners, the homeless, and students living in poverty.

Even in schools with adequate computer resources for students, access is an issue. Unlimited student access to computers cannot be allowed by schools for a number of reasons, many of which are discussed in this book. At a minimum, schools must monitor students using school computer resources. Schools generally fulfill this monitoring obligation by prohibiting certain student uses of the Internet and filtering or blocking Internet content.

ACCESS, FILTERING, AND THE LAW

As Patricia First and Yolanda Hart (2002) state in their article, "Access to Cyberspace: The New Issue in Educational Justice," the **digital divide** is the new measure separating society into haves and have-nots. A number of other scholars share their concern. The first two scenarios above show that Native American and rural communities are especially hard-hit. Constrained by geography and lack of infrastructure, the Navajo nation has no alternative Internet-access mechanism or Internet provider. Access can be denied with the flip of a switch. The rural Arkansas school in the second example came up with a creative way of providing students with an Internet experience during their long commute to and from school, but expansion of the program to other students depends on financial contributions from the private sector.

Other groups with historically poor access to technology include African Americans, Hispanics, those living in poverty, and the disabled. Statistically speaking, students in these groups are less likely to have computers and Internet access in their homes. It is vital that these students have access to computers and the Internet in school. The technology around which much of our nation's educational system is becoming based must at least be equally available to students in all schools. Internet use is becoming central to life in the United States. Colleges and universities expect entering students to have basic computing skills, and workers with computer skills or who work in industries in which computers are used extensively are paid higher wages and have greater opportunity for advancement.

The third example above raises a different kind of access issue. In this example, the high-school student accessed sexually explicit material. It may be, in this instance, that the school involved was not using **filtering software** or that the filters were set to a low threshold, something that arguably makes sense in a high-school setting even if it does increase the likelihood of students accessing inappropriate material. The school may also be one of many schools that choose to address student computer and access via policy. In that case, if the student intentionally accessed the material, he likely will be disciplined. Whether the librarian also may be disciplined is less clear and would depend on the level of monitoring the school promised parents, the length of time the student spent accessing inappropriate material, and whether the students who witnessed the downloading had an obligation to report it.

Although many people in the educational arena debate the benefits of filtering, filtering is a reality for most public schools. In 2000, **the Children's Internet Protection Act (CIPA)** was signed into law. Among other things, CIPA includes a mandate that public schools install filtering software to be eligible to receive federal **E-Rate** funding. The law does not specifically state what content must be filtered, just that filtering software must be installed and used. Accordingly, schools need to be knowledgeable about filtering, understand how it works, and make sound decisions about what and when to filter.

Many schools mistakenly allow outside vendors to set the parameters of their filtering software. Other schools take responsibility for filtering decisions but fail to adjust filters to suit the needs of students and teachers based on grade level or subject matter. When schools overfilter, they risk impeding the educational efforts of their teaching staffs. They may also risk lawsuits. Although there are no current court cases relating to filtering in schools, there are potential constitutional problems relating to the installation of filtering software, particularly if the software screens out too much. Conversely, when schools do not filter adequately and students gain access to inappropriate or harmful materials, schools may be accused of being negligent and be at risk of lawsuits by parents who allege their children were harmed by accessed materials.

Ideally, schools should customize their filtering approaches, and then monitor the effectiveness of their filtering approaches. Teacher feedback and periodic checks by the school's information technology (IT) staff can help schools fine tune their filtering decisions. Incidents like that described in the third scenario above highlight the need for filters but also the need for a Plan B. Simply stated, filtering does not always work. Even the most finely tuned filtering software is not foolproof.

As Nancy Willard (2000) points out in her article, "Legal and Ethical Issues Related to the Use of the Internet in K–12 Schools," schools should not rely on filtering software alone.

Reliance on filtering software does not prepare a young person for the inevitable time that he or she will have unsupervised and unfiltered access to the Internet. Schools that rely on filtering frequently do not address the search skills that young people can use to avoid inadvertently accessing this kind of material, nor do they discuss issues around the dark side of the Internet and the need to make responsible choices. Schools that rely on filtering can become complacent about monitoring, thus leading to other problems (258).

Student Internet access is not just an issue for schools. It is a matter of concern for legislators too. Internet safety was cited as a key issue for states at the 2007 National Governors Association meeting. Some states have enacted legislation requiring that schools provide Internet safety instruction, at least for those students involved in online-educational programs.

Internet safety is the frequent focus of federal legislators as well. The *Protecting Children in the 21st Century Act* (S. 49) was introduced in the U.S. Senate in 2007. A related bill by the same name (S. 1965) was passed by the Senate with amendments by unanimous consent in May of 2008. The amended bill requires schools receiving federal E-Rate funds to educate students about Internet safety, including how to interact on social-networking sites and in chat rooms and how to recognize and respond to cyberbullying.

In commenting on this proposed legislation, Don Knezek, CEO of the International Society for Technology in Education, stated, "One of a school's primary functions is to ensure safety and build responsible citizens, and trying to block every threatening activity that goes on in society is not a formula for effective education." Knezek and others praised the bill as a "common-sense" approach to keeping kids safe online that is far superior to Congress's earlier legislative attempts, which were criticized for being too broad and which likely would have prevented educators from taking full advantage of the Internet as a tool for teaching and learning (Knezek quoted in Goldmann, 2007–2008).

THE ROLE OF THE SCHOOLS

Although schools cannot single handedly solve the problem of the digital divide, schools can provide students without home access to computers with a rich computer and Internet experience. Schools can build computing skills into their curricula, starting with the youngest students. They can be choosy about the software programs they purchase for use in the classroom, ensuring that programs that require critical-thinking skills and use of the Internet are available to students, not just drill and practice software.

Schools and nonprofit groups also can support computer take-home programs, laptop initiatives, computer literacy programs, and the donation of refurbished computers to families in need. The University of Pennsylvania program that operated from 2000 to 2008 and served the West Philadelphia community offers an excellent model for schools. The program not only refurbished discarded and donated computers for community computer labs but arranged for university students to teach youth and adult computer literacy classes, work in after-school programs, and provide technical support and curriculum development to classroom teachers. An initiative in Miami, Florida, funded by grants and partnerships with the Miami business community provides another model. Sixth graders in Miami public schools can earn laptop computers by achieving above-average attendance and good grades and demonstrating good manners.

With regard to filtering, schools should strive for a balanced approach. As Robert Ashmore states in his 2006 article, "Blocking 'MySpace' From Your Space," schools need to provide sufficient access so students can "mine useful Internet resources," but must also protect students from the Internet's "dangers and distractions."

Ashmore's Recommended Approaches to Filtering

- Don't go overboard in what you block.
- Don't cede your blocking authority to technology staff.
- Include an unblocking procedure.
- Communicate your decisions and expectations.
- Require parental permission.
- Don't try to control out-of-school access.

Source: Ashmore, R. W. (2006). Blocking "My Space" from your space. *School Administrator, 63*(9), 7.

Schools should be clear in their filtering decisions, their written policies, and their classroom instruction that there are categories of material that clearly may not be accessed (e.g., profane, obscene, and sexually explicit material; material that advocates violence, drug use, or other dangerous acts; and hate literature) and that students, teachers, and staff are required to report instances in which such materials are accessed, whether intentionally or inadvertently. Schools should also provide staff monitoring of students, in addition to filtering and blocking, but should ensure that parents understand that the school may not be able to monitor all instances of computer access and certainly will not be able to monitor students in accord with a multitude of different family values.

Sample Policy Language—Inappropriate Access to Material

V. Unacceptable Uses

A. The following uses of the school district system and Internet resources or accounts are considered unacceptable:

1. Users will not use the school district system to access, review, upload, download, store, print, post, receive, transmit or distribute:

   a. pornographic, obscene or sexually explicit material or other visual depictions;

   b. obscene, abusive, profane, lewd, vulgar, rude, inflammatory, threatening, disrespectful, or sexually explicit language;

   c. materials that use language or images that are inappropriate in the education setting or disruptive to the educational process;

   d. materials that use language or images that advocate violence or discrimination toward other people (hate literature) or that may constitute harassment or discrimination or threatens the safety of others.

B. If a user inadvertently accesses unacceptable materials or an unacceptable Internet site, the user shall immediately disclose the inadvertent access to an appropriate school district official. In the case of a school district employee, the immediate disclosure shall be to the employee's immediate supervisor and/or the building administrator. In the case of a student, the immediate disclosure shall be made to the classroom teacher or building principal. This disclosure may serve as a defense against an allegation that the user has intentionally violated this policy. In certain rare instances, a user also may access otherwise unacceptable materials if necessary to complete an assignment and if done with the prior approval of and with appropriate guidance from the appropriate teacher or, in the case of a school district employee, the building administrator.

VI. Filter

A. With respect to any of its computers with Internet access, the school district will follow the guidelines provided by the Children's Internet Protection Act of 2001 (CIPA), and will monitor the online activities of minors and employ technology protection measures during any use of such computers by minors and adults.

The technology protection measures utilized will block or filter Internet access to any visual depictions that are:

1. obscene

2. child pornography
3. harmful to minors

B. The term "harmful to minors" means any picture, image, graphic image file, or other visual depiction that:

1. Taken as a whole and with respect to minors, appeals to a prurient interest in nudity, sex, or excretion; or

2. Depicts, describes, or represents, in a patently offensive way with respect to what is suitable for minors, an actual or simulated sexual act or sexual contact, actual or simulated normal or perverted sexual acts, or a lewd exhibition of the genitals; and

3. Taken as a whole, lacks serious literary, artistic, political, or scientific value as to minors.

C. An administrator, supervisor or other person authorized by the superintendent may disable the technology protection measure, during use by an adult, to enable access for bona fide research or other lawful purposes.

Source: Internet Acceptable Use and Safety Policy (Policy 524), Edina Public Schools.

Because filtering alone is not sufficient to guard against students' accessing inappropriate materials, schools also must provide education about responsible Internet use. Classroom instruction about how to access and use the Internet must be comprehensive, as students will carry their classroom instruction about Internet safety with them as they access computers in unsupervised settings and settings in which access to the Internet is not filtered.

Teachers can help students safely navigate the Internet by customizing classroom assignments to match the age and experience of the students. Teachers of younger students will likely want to restrict students' in-class access to Web sites the teacher already has visited and determined to be reliable, both from the standpoint of accuracy and safety. For older students, teachers can provide recommended sites or lists of resources prepared by educational groups to guide student research. Some textbook publishers offer supporting Web sites, and teachers should take advantage of these.

Teachers should also provide direct instruction on Internet safety. Internet safety topics should include how to conduct Internet searches that minimize the likelihood of accessing inappropriate material; what to do when inappropriate material is accessed; and the importance of reporting sexual, threatening, or other inappropriate online contact. For example, instead of banning social-networking sites outright, teachers should spend time with students discussing appropriate posting to such sites, why students should not share personal information on such sites in a flirtatious or sexually suggestive way, and the staying power of any information posted to the Internet.

Whether at home, at a public library, at a friend's house, or even on a school computer on which filtering software is not installed, it is critical that students understand how to recognize inappropriate content and how to respond.

CONCLUSION

Access to technology is a critical issue for today's students. Computer and Internet skills are no longer *nice-to-have* skills but are *need-to-have* skills, essential to the operation of our governments, businesses, and schools. For schools to adequately train today's students for tomorrow's world, schools need the technology and funding to ensure access to all schools. Managing student use of technology once computers are in the schools presents another type of access issue, but one that is much more easily managed with effective policy, supervision, and filtering software.

Checklist Regarding Access and Filtering

Has your district done the following?

☐ **Assessed whether your school's curricula adequately bridges the digital divide?** It is essential that schools teach computing skills to all students. Many businesses and nonprofit entities may be willing to partner with schools to help bring greater computer access and training to students.

☐ **Established a well-conceived, balanced Internet use and filtering policy?** Schools should be clear in their written policies, classroom instruction, and filtering policies that certain categories of materials (e.g., profane, obscene, and sexually explicit material; material that advocates violence, drug use, or other dangerous acts; hate literature) clearly may not be accessed. Determine how and to what

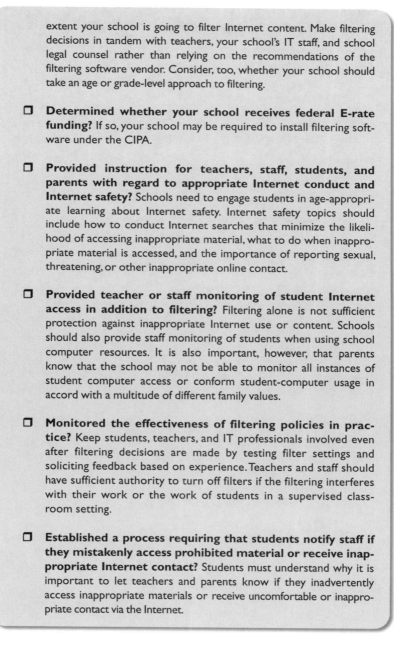

extent your school is going to filter Internet content. Make filtering decisions in tandem with teachers, your school's IT staff, and school legal counsel rather than relying on the recommendations of the filtering software vendor. Consider, too, whether your school should take an age or grade-level approach to filtering.

☐ **Determined whether your school receives federal E-rate funding?** If so, your school may be required to install filtering software under the CIPA.

☐ **Provided instruction for teachers, staff, students, and parents with regard to appropriate Internet conduct and Internet safety?** Schools need to engage students in age-appropriate learning about Internet safety. Internet safety topics should include how to conduct Internet searches that minimize the likelihood of accessing inappropriate material, what to do when inappropriate material is accessed, and the importance of reporting sexual, threatening, or other inappropriate online contact.

☐ **Provided teacher or staff monitoring of student Internet access in addition to filtering?** Filtering alone is not sufficient protection against inappropriate Internet use or content. Schools should also provide staff monitoring of students when using school computer resources. It is also important, however, that parents know that the school may not be able to monitor all instances of student computer access or conform student-computer usage in accord with a multitude of different family values.

☐ **Monitored the effectiveness of filtering policies in practice?** Keep students, teachers, and IT professionals involved even after filtering decisions are made by testing filter settings and soliciting feedback based on experience. Teachers and staff should have sufficient authority to turn off filters if the filtering interferes with their work or the work of students in a supervised classroom setting.

☐ **Established a process requiring that students notify staff if they mistakenly access prohibited material or receive inappropriate Internet contact?** Students must understand why it is important to let teachers and parents know if they inadvertently access inappropriate materials or receive uncomfortable or inappropriate contact via the Internet.

Online Resources

Children and the Internet: Policies That Work.

http://www.ala.org/ala/mgrps/divs/alsc/issuesadv/internettech/childrentheinternetpoliciesthatwork/index.cfm

Cyber Smart!

http://www.cybersmartcurriculum.org/home

Filtering Facts.

http://filteringfacts.org/

iKeepSafe.org.

http://ikeepsafe.org/

iSafe.org.

http://isafe.org/

CHAPTER SIX

Copyright Law in the Classroom

Steering Clear of Legal Liability

A school district in California was sued for making nearly 1,400 unauthorized copies of Adobe Photoshop and Microsoft Word and installing them on district computers. The law suit eventually settled out of court, with the school district paying a fine of $300,000 plus the cost of replacing the illegal copies districtwide, roughly $5 million.

A Texas school administrator made 300 copies of multiple pages from a book and distributed them at a districtwide meeting. The administrator was warned against making the copies without permission but did so anyway. The publisher of the book was made aware of the copying and sent cease-and-desist letters to the administrator and the superintendent and demanded payment in an amount equal to 300 copies of the book, which reportedly was $15,000.

The American Society of Composers, Authors, and Publishers (ASCAP), the organization that represents the interests of songwriters, sent a mailing to 6,000 Girl Scout camps demanding payment of performance royalties by scouts for singing copyrighted songs at camp. Included in the mailing was a schedule of fees that went as high as $1,400 for large, year-round camps. ASCAP argued that singing any of its more than 4 million copyrighted songs without payment of royalties constituted unauthorized performance of copyrighted works by the scouts. When news of ASCAP's demands hit the mainstream media, ASCAP quickly backed off of its legal claim.

U.S. **copyright** law affects schools in a multitude of ways. Increased opportunities for copyright violations (called infringement) arise when computers, digital recording devices, digital cameras, and the Internet are used by students and teachers because of the ease with which others' copyrighted material can be accessed, copied, and reused. Many educational uses of copyrighted material fall within the fair-use exception to copyright, a portion of the statute that provides for use of some copyrighted materials without permission, but the mere fact that students and teachers are using copyrighted works in educational settings does not, in itself, exempt them from liability under copyright law. A great deal of information on the Internet is protected by copyright, and contrary to popular belief, there is no blanket exception under copyright law for educational uses of that information.

COPYRIGHT LAW

What is protected by copyright? Copyright law protects *original works* of authorship fixed in a *tangible medium* of expression. Original works of authorship include many things: literary works; musical works, including any accompanying words; dramatic works, including any accompanying music; pantomimes and choreographic works; pictorial, graphic, and sculptural works; motion pictures and other audiovisual works; sound recordings; and architectural works. The works are fixed in a tangible medium when they are written, drawn, recorded, or otherwise captured in a way that others can see, hear, feel, or copy them.

Copyrighted works do not lose their copyright protection when they are posted to the Internet (e.g., music files, YouTube videos, FaceBook photographs), something that can be difficult for students to understand. The right to display or to perform a copyrighted work belongs solely to the copyright owner (see the ASCAP scenario above). In fact, copyright owners are granted a number of exclusive rights: the right to reproduce their work (such as when photocopies are made); the right to distribute their work; the right to create derivative works, which are new works based in whole or in part on the original work (such as a screenplay-based on a novel); the right to publicly display their work; the right to publicly perform their work (whether for free or for commercial gain); and, in the case of sound recordings, the right to publicly perform the work by means of a digital audio transmission. Anyone else wishing to make use of a copyrighted work must first seek permission from the copyright owner.

What are some common ways students and teachers infringe on others' copyrights? They photocopy others' written works or drawings. They publicly perform copyrighted works without permission or paying a licensing fee. They download documents or images from the Internet. They post others' written or graphic works to their own Web site or use them in their own presentations or multimedia projects. Doing any of these things without the permission of the copyright owner may constitute infringement for which both the student or teacher *and the school* can be held liable. As the first scenario above illustrates, fines for infringement can run into the thousands of dollars.

FAIR USE

So, what about fair use? Isn't fair use available as a defense to a lot of infringing activity in the educational arena? The answer is, "it depends." Fair use often can be asserted in educational settings. In determining whether a use of someone else's copyrighted work without their permission qualifies as a fair use under the copyright law, four factors must be evaluated:

1. The purpose for which the work is used (nonprofit, teaching, and research uses generally are allowed, whereas commercial uses generally are not)

2. The nature or characteristics of the work (The use of published or nonfiction works generally is favored over the use of unpublished or fictional, highly creative works because, in the case of the latter, the author either did not agree to share the work publicly via publication or the highly creative nature of the work makes it more unique than a collection of facts that could be amassed by any researcher.)

3. The amount and substantiality of the work used (which includes an evaluation of the quality and the quantity of the work used, so using large portions of a work or portions of the work that are considered key or central to the work is not permitted)

4. The effect of the use on the marketability or value of the work (If the use negatively affects the sale or value of the work, it is rarely allowed, so it is important to limit the number of copies made and to not engage in repeated or long-term use of the work without obtaining permission.)

Applying the four factors can be difficult. Copyright law does not provide hard-and-fast rules about how much of a copyrighted work may be used without permission. It does not delineate how many lines of a copyrighted poem may be used or how many minutes of a copyrighted song may be played. Accordingly, although fair use sometimes is available as a defense to infringement, schools seeking to reduce the likelihood of copyright violations must think strategically. Occasionally relying on fair use as a rationale to use another's work without permission (assuming you've done a good faith analysis of your use using the above factors) may not be a problem if schools make an effort to reduce infringing activity overall by providing sufficient classroom resources (e.g., licensed clip art collections, classroom subscriptions to online databases or periodicals, and royalty-free music collections) so that teachers do not have to frequently go outside the classroom for material. Blatant infringement, however, such as is described in the first two scenarios above, can never be supported with a fair-use argument.

THE ROLE OF THE SCHOOLS

How can schools reduce the risk of **copyright infringement** in the classroom? The key ingredient to avoiding claims of infringement is for schools to understand the law and the need to contact copyright owners to negotiate the terms under which the schools may use the copyrighted works. In some instances, merely contacting the copyright owner will result in permission being given by the owner for use of the copyrighted work by the school. In other instances, negotiation will be required. These negotiations may result in the school making payments to the copyright owners, in exchange for which the schools are permitted to exercise some of the copyright owner's exclusive rights (e.g., photocopying and distributing the copyrighted works to students).

Schools also need to educate students, teachers, and staff. Specifically, they need to communicate licensing and permissions information to those students, teachers, and staff who will use the copyrighted works. Whether purchasing software for school computers, sheet music for the school orchestra, or performance rights for the student musical, schools must ensure that all members of the school community are aware of and honor the terms of their agreements with the copyright owners. These agreements are called licenses, and their terms can vary greatly from copyright owner to copyright owner with regard to who is permitted to use the material, the use that can be made of the material, and the length of time the material may be used. Students, teachers, and staff need to understand the need to obtain licenses and when and how they can use licensed material legally.

Tips on Obtaining a License to Use a Copyrighted Work

Schools can avoid claims of infringement by obtaining a license (i.e., getting permission) to use copyrighted works. Whether crafting your own letter or using a form provided by the copyright owner, strive to do the following:

1. **Identify the work.** Provide the owner with specifics (for example, the title, date of publication, and location of publisher) about the work you want to use and whether you want to use the entire work or only a portion.

2. **Identify your audience.** Provide the copyright owner with information about *how many people* will use or view the work or *how many copies* you intend to produce.

3. **Identify when and how long you want to use the work.** State whether you intend to use the work only briefly or whether you would like continuing permission to use the work for a longer period of time. If you want to use the work for a specific period of time, specifically identify the time period (permission fees generally are tied directly to the length of time you want to use the work).

4. **Identify your purpose.** Provide the owner with information about why you want to use the work and whether your intended use is commercial, nonprofit, or educational.

5. **Identify the context within which you want to use the work.** Provide the owner with information about how and where the work will be used (for example, whether the work will be used by students in a classroom setting or performed by students for the community, as a spring musical).

6. **Be flexible and accommodating.** Provide the owner with information about how to reach you (at no expense to the owner) and state that you are willing to abide by the owner's restrictions (e.g., the owner may insist on certain terms regarding use of the work, access to the work, size and placement of the credit line, and so on).

Schools have other options as well. Schools can purchase collections of royalty-free music and clip art for use by students and teachers, take advantage of open-source software, subscribe to news services whose licenses allow for classroom copying and distribution, create or subscribe to **learning object repositories,** and introduce teachers to **OpenCourseWare** sites that provide a variety of resources developed by major colleges and universities around the world free for use by teachers. School legal counsel can approve safe haven guidelines for teachers and staff relating to classroom use of copyrighted materials along the lines of the guidelines proffered by the Association of Research Libraries.

Know Your Copy Rights™

Often you can use works in your teaching without permission or fee.
This chart highlights some of those situations. However, there are other circumstances where permission and/or fee are required (for example, when some types of works are included in course packs). Check with your institution's library or legal office for information about campus copyright policies.

What You Can Do

			Proposed Use			
			Exhibit materials in a live classroom?	Post materials to an online class?	Distribute readings?	Create electronic reserves?
Legal Status of Work To Be Used	Works Not Copyrighted	**Public Domain Works** (US Govt. and pre-1923 works, and certain other works)	Yes	Yes	Yes	Yes
		Your Own Works (if you kept copyright or reserved use rights)	Yes	Yes	Yes	Yes
	Copyrighted Works	**Open Access Works** (works available online without license, password, or technical restrictions)	Yes	Link	Link	Link
		Electronic Works Licensed by Your Institution (depends on license, but usually permitted)	Yes	Link	Link (Most licenses also allow students to make an individual copy.)	Link
		Electronic Works with a Creative Commons License (depends on license, but usually permitted; if not, LINK)	Yes	Yes	Yes	Yes
		Other Works (when none of above apply)	Yes	Yes, if meets either TEACH Act or Fair Use standards. If not, LINK or seek permission.	Yes, if meets Fair Use standards. If not, LINK or seek permission.	Yes, if meets Fair Use standards. If not, LINK or seek permission.

Brought to you by your institution's library and

ASSOCIATION OF RESEARCH LIBRARIES
www.arl.org

This chart and other instructive materials can be obtained free of charge from the Association of Research Libraries at www.knowyourcopyrights.org/index .shtml.

PUBLIC DOMAIN

One easy approach to reducing the risk of infringement is to educate students and teachers about **public domain** materials. Public domain materials are not eligible for copyright protection, so there are no copyright restrictions on the use, photocopying, and performance of public domain materials (unless the materials are protected by another intellectual property law, as in the case of trademark, for example). Works in the public domain include works that never were copyrightable, as well as works for which the copyright has expired. They include the following:

> **Government publications.** Works prepared by an officer or an employee of the U.S. government as a part of that person's official duty are not copyrightable. For example, photos taken by NASA scientists of planets or the space station and posted to the NASA Web site may be copied and used by students in reports or presentations.
>
> **Works excluded from protection by statute.** Sometimes, copyrighted works may be used without permission because the particular use being made of them falls within a statutory exception to the copyright law, such as fair use or the Technology, Education, and Copyright Harmonization Act (TEACH Act), the exception to copyright law that deals with the use of copyrighted materials in distance education. For example, a teacher's copying and distribution to students on one occasion of a current article on a topic being covered in class would qualify as a noninfringing use under the fair use exception.
>
> **Works for which copyright protection has expired.** The duration of copyright protection for any particular work depends on the law in effect at the time of the work's creation. At a minimum, this refers to all works created before 1923, which explains, for instance, why there are so many versions of *The Night Before Christmas* available in libraries. The copyright on the poem by Sir Clement Moore has expired, so others are free to change it, illustrate it, and produce their own copyrighted versions of it.

Educating about public domain materials and encouraging use of public domain materials in school assignments, projects, and curriculum plans is an effective way to reduce the risk of copyright infringement.

LEARNING OBJECT REPOSITORIES

Restricting classroom use to public domain materials is not the only way to reduce the risk of infringement. Learning object repositories are

Free Online, Interactive Tutorials on Copyright Law That Can Be Used by Students, Staff, and Teachers

1. University of Maryland's Copyright Primer (including an interactive 21 question quiz) at http://www-apps.umuc.edu/primer/enter.php#

2. University of Texas's Crash Course in Copyright at http://www.utsystem.edu/ogc/intellectualproperty/cprtindx.htm

3. Minnesota State Colleges and Universities' Copyright Web site (including "check your understanding" scenarios about educational copyright issues) at http://www.copyright.mnscu.edu/

another helpful tool. Learning object repositories are online databases of learning content. The content they contain (the learning objects) can range from short paragraphs on specific subjects to complete classroom plans or online courses.

Learning object repositories vary with regard to the content they provide. Some are wide ranging in the content areas they cover. For example, the Multimedia Educational Resource for Learning and Online Teaching (MERLOT) provides links to online learning materials in academic areas ranging from biology to business to criminal justice, world languages, and engineering. MERLOT also has a special "faculty development portal" for teachers.

Other learning object repositories focus on specific topics. One example of a topic specific repository is Scivee, which offers science related videos and podcasts. Described as an "online science community where scientists can make their research known to their fellow peers as well as the general public," Scivee is loaded with online presentations that can be used by students and teachers.

Learning object repositories provide access to a wealth of materials, many of which are available with no restrictions when used in educational settings. This makes learning object repositories good tools for reducing the risk of infringement in the classroom.

OPENCOURSEWARE

As defined by the OpenCourseWare Consortium, OpenCourseWare is "a free and open digital publication of high-quality educational materials, organized as courses." More than 100 institutions of higher education and related organizations from around the world comprise the Consortium. Each Consortium member hosts a Web site with content from a minimum of 10 courses. The content is offered without cost to students and teachers.

Although the majority of Consortium members post college-level courses on their OpenCourseWare sites, a great deal of the posted content is applicable in the K–12 setting. Moreover, as the OpenCourseWare phenomenon grows, it is likely that K–12 content will become more plentiful. The Massachusetts Institute of Technology (MIT), a leader in the OpenCourseWare movement, unveiled one of the first sites aimed at high-school students and teachers in 2007. The site, Highlights for High School, offers free online resources designed to improve science, technology, engineering, and math instruction at the high-school level. Included among those resources are more than 2,600 video and audio clips, animations, lecture notes, and assignments taken from actual MIT courses, organized to match advanced placement course curricula.

OpenCourseWare sites are specifically designed with educators in mind. They provide quality content and eliminate the need for students and teachers to seek permission and negotiate licenses.

Classroom Materials With No Copyright Strings Attached

1. **Learning object repositories**. These free, online, searchable collections offer learning objects to faculty and students in nonprofit, educational settings. Learning objects include policy guides, simulations, tutorials, scholarly papers, and multimedia presentations. The terms under which the learning objects may be used vary from object to object but, in most cases, no royalties or permissions are required for classroom use.

2. **OpenCourseWare (OCW)**. OpenCourseWare sites are offered by colleges and universities from around the world. They offer free and open access to high-quality educational materials, organized as courses. Course information may be downloaded and adapted for classroom use by teachers and students. For more information about course offerings and participating colleges and universities, go to the OpenCourseWare Consortium Web site at http://www.ocwconsor tium.org/.

3. **Creative Commons. Creative Commons** is sponsored by a nonprofit group. It provides a free copyright licensing framework that allows authors, scientists, artists, and educators to easily identify the uses they are willing to let others make of their work. The Creative Commons Web site can be found at http://creativecommons.org/.

(Continued)

(Continued)

4. **Open source software.** Open source computer software is free and, perhaps more important, may be studied, copied, modified, and redistributed. One popular source of open source software is GNU. GNU's free software directory has a specific education listing, with separate elementary and secondary education categories. GNU can be found at http://www.gnu.org.

5. **Open source course management systems.** These free computer software packages help educators create online learning communities. One such software package popular among educators is *Moodle*, which offers an array of features including forums, quizzes, blogs, wikis, surveys, and multilingual support. For more information on *Moodle*, including course demonstrations, go to http://moodle .org/.

CREATIVE COMMONS

In their efforts to reduce the risk of infringement, schools should also acquaint students, teachers, and staff with Creative Commons licensing. Creative Commons is an alternative to traditional copyright licensing. Founded by a group of cyber law and intellectual property experts, Creative Commons provides a licensing scheme whereby copyright owners choose the terms under which they will allow use of their copyrighted works and make that choice known via the use of easily identifiable logos.

Copyright owners who are willing to share their works with others can choose from several different Creative Commons licensing levels (attribution, noncommercial, no derivatives, and share alike). In doing so, they can offer some rights to their copyrighted works to the public without risk of giving up other rights. Students, teachers, and staff can seek out and use copyrighted works licensed under Creative Commons without fear of infringement because Creative Commons allows them to know, at a glance, which works they are free to use and under what conditions.

Creative Commons

Works licensed under Creative Commons are identified by this logo.

The different levels of Creative Commons licensing and their accompanying logos are as follows:

Attribution. Attribution means users must keep intact any copyright notices for the works they want to use, credit the copyright owner and all other parties specified by the copyright owner, use the correct title of the work, and include the uniform resource identifier for the work (if requested by the copyright owner).

Noncommercial. Noncommercial means users may not use the work to gain a direct commercial advantage or as part of a private money-making venture.

No derivatives. No derivatives means users may not adapt and change the work. They may only use the work in its original form or verbiage.

Share alike. Share alike means users may adapt and change the work (i.e., create derivative works) but only if they agree to license their new works under the same Creative Commons licensing scheme as the original work.

For more information, go to Creative Commons, http://creative commons .org/.

Creative Commons licensing reduces the risk of copyright infringement in the classroom because, as long as the copyright owners' Creative Commons terms are honored, there is no need to seek permission to use a copyrighted work or to worry about whether use of the work falls within the fair use exception to the copyright law. Users only need to contact copyright owners for permission to use certain works if their proposed use is not a permitted use under the terms of the Creative Commons license.

CONCLUSION

In short, copyright law, though detailed, is not unmanageable. Online tutorials and information packed Web sites are available to help educate students and teachers about copyright issues. Alternatives to traditional copyright licensing approaches are available, and the number of alternatives continues to increase. School leaders do not need to feel hog-tied by copyright law, but they do need to accept the responsibility of educating all users of the school Internet system about legal uses of copyrighted material and how to steer clear of infringement.

Checklist for Reducing Copyright Infringement

Has your district done the following?

☐ **Addressed copyright infringement directly?** Does your district have an updated copyright compliance policy? Is use of copyrighted materials monitored? Make sure your policy identifies when permission is necessary. Provide a sample permission request form. Enlist your district's legal counsel to draft guidelines for conducting a fair use analysis. Monitor computer labs and school publications, notices, and postings for copyright violations.

☐ **Provided students, teachers, and staff with sufficient opportunity to request and obtain copyrighted materials?** Is someone within the district responsible for coordinating the purchase and use of copyrighted materials? Are licensing agreements kept in a central location and available for review by users of the copyrighted materials? Districts need to provide teachers and staff with regular opportunities to request materials. They need to allocate money in the district budget for these licenses and buy performance rights for theater, band, orchestra, and choral teachers; curriculum-related DVDs and videos and licensed collections of music and images for classroom teachers; and sufficient copies of software for computer labs.

☐ **Educated members of the school community about copyright?** Has your district conducted teacher and staff development on copyright? Does your district's Internet education curriculum include sections on copyright? Are copyright discussions integrated into regular classroom teaching? Districts should provide teachers and staff with a list of authoritative copyright resources; provide students with a list of student friendly copyright resources, including online tutorials; and create links to copyright resource information on district Web sites that parents can access.

Online Resources

Copyright Basics. United States Copyright Office.
   http://www.copyright.gov/circs/circ1.html

Copyright and Intellectual Property, Minnesota State Colleges & Universities.
   http://orpheum.its.mnscu.edu/copyright/college/index.html

Campus Alberta Repository of Educational Objects (CAREO).
   http://www.ucalgary.ca/commons/careo/CAREOrepo.htm

Multimedia Educational Resource for Learning and Online Teaching (MERLOT).
   http://www.merlot.org/merlot/index.htm

CHAPTER SEVEN

Policies, Procedures, and Contracts

Communicating Expectations to Teachers, Students, and Parents

A middle school has a zero-tolerance, "no-cell-phones-in-the-classroom" policy. Students are permitted to have cell phones at school but must keep them turned-off and in their lockers except for before and after school and during lunch. A few students have parents deployed overseas with the military. Because those parents have little control over when they can call their children, the principal has made an exception and allowed their children to keep cell phones with them in class, as long as they are set on vibrate. The parent of another student is in prison and can only call her child during school hours. The principal has made an exception for this child as well. Several parents learned about the exceptions the principal has made for these children and are now demanding that their children also be allowed to have their cell phones in the classroom.

A high school without a written policy on student organization Web pages is experiencing an increase in the number of requests for dedicated space on the district Web page from various student groups so that they can create Web pages for their clubs and teams. The school has granted similar requests in the past to the football and baseball teams. Those teams created Web pages and posted their rosters, schedules, and league standings. However, the most recent request for space is of some concern to the principal. The request is from the high school's gay-straight alliance, a group of students without official high-school club status.

A middle-school teacher moonlights as a stand-up comic at a local comedy club. By all reports, the teacher's routine is quite funny, but it includes a number of off-color jokes about fictional students and life as a public school teacher. Members of the school board have met and discussed the matter. They understand that the teacher has the right to pursue stand-up comedy, but they wonder what, if any, restrictions they can require him to place on his routine.

Acceptable use policies (AUPs), bullying policies, parent permission slips, photographic releases, disciplinary procedures—all of these, and more, are used by schools to define the rights and responsibilities of students, teachers, and staff. Although they vary in form, length, and content, all are contracts and all are binding on the members of the school community.

Contracts, in essence, establish the *private law* developed by and between parties to address specific situations and relationships. Contracts allow parties to create their own rules of the game. Parties can use contracts to define the terms under which they will work together. Parties also can change those terms (i.e., can amend their contracts) if changing the terms makes sense in light of changing circumstances. It is the flexibility of contracts that makes them ideally suited to handling technology issues, particularly those issues relating to student, teacher, and staff use of school computers and the school Internet system.

CONTRACT LAW

At first blush, the term *contract* may bring to mind multipage, form business agreements, thick with fine print and boilerplate language. But school handbooks, school policies, even simple parent permission slips are all contracts. In fact, school policies may be the most widely used contracts between schools and the members of their school communities. Well-crafted policies lay out expectations, define rights and responsibilities, describe procedures, and detail the remedies available if the policy is violated. Policies allow administrators to use contract-law principles to create a type of private law that governs the school community.

Contracts can be customized to address particular situations and to serve the needs of different groups. For example, a school district may draft one district-wide Internet use policy for its students but, within that policy, may prescribe different disciplinary sanctions for violations of the policy based on the grade level of potential offenders. As another example, a school district with a long-standing antibullying policy may, based on its finding of an increase in offensive text messaging and e-mailing among students, amend its policy to include a prohibition against cyberbullying. Contract law allows school leaders to tailor school rules to their particular school settings.

School leaders craft the policies they think are appropriate (often with the assistance of legal counsel), put students and parents on notice of the school's contract terms by publishing and distributing the policies, and require parents and students to return signed permission or acknowledgment forms before student privileges are granted. School policies, in essence, become the law of the school district, albeit a flexible kind of law that can be revisited and amended as needed to fit the ever changing needs of the school district. In the first example above, for instance, the middle school has a written policy relating to cell phones. It appears, though, that given the increase in military deployments in recent years, the policy may need to be modified. The flexibility of contract law permits this.

School AUPs are the primary vehicles for establishing private law for school communities on the issues of use of school computers and the school Internet system. AUPs vary greatly from school to school. They are all similar, though, in that they lay out the terms and conditions surrounding the use of school computer and Internet resources; describe student, teacher, and staff privileges; prescribe rules of behavior; and identify the consequences for violating those rules. They can be customized to provide varying privileges depending on user age, grade level, or user status (student versus teacher) and can require participation in mandatory training before user privileges are extended. Perhaps most notably, they can be revisited and amended as often as the school deems necessary, which makes it possible to incorporate new technology.

Resource Alert!

A sample AUP is included in Resource B in this book. Additional online resources relating to AUPs and policy drafting guidelines are also included at the end of this chapter.

The district in the second example needs to amend its AUP. Given the increasing number of requests, the district must establish a policy relating to student organization Web pages. Consultation with legal counsel will reveal that the district essentially has three options: (1) It can draft a policy that establishes viewpoint-neutral standards for student organization Web pages (i.e., standards that require that posted material relate specifically to organization activities and programs); (2) it can draft a policy that prohibits student organization Web pages entirely; or (3) it can draft a policy that permits student organization Web pages, with the only restriction being that the Web pages must comply with district communication rules and school rules. Once the district has determined the direction it wants to go, it can proceed with amending its AUP.

School records retention policies also are contracts. Records retention policies address the storage, retention, and destruction of electronic records created and stored on school computers and Internet systems. These records include student grade reports, attendance records, standardized test scores, and other student-specific information, as well as information related to the school as a whole.

Records retention policies are even more important now, because of a December 2006 change to the Federal Rules of Civil Procedure. Although electronic records have been used as evidence in lawsuits for over a decade, the change to the Federal Rules formalized the status of electronic records in federal lawsuits. A school's failure to preserve electronic records necessary to a lawsuit can now result in harsh sanctions against the school and its legal counsel. These sanctions can include financial penalties, exclusion of witnesses or pleadings, adverse inference instructions, dismissals, and default judgments.

Because, under the amended rules, schools no longer can allow haphazard storing or purging of electronic records, a contract law solution must be crafted. Schools, working with legal counsel, need to draft records retention policies appropriate for their schools and policies that fit their schools' needs and operating plans, while still providing adequate direction and protection for the information technology (IT) professionals charged with records oversight. Just as with the AUPs above, the policies drafted by different schools likely will vary from school to school. The flexibility of contract law is necessary for this scenario in which the law is expected to continue to evolve.

Throughout the earlier chapters of this book, there are references to a variety of school policies. Chapters 1 and 2 discuss the need for policies on cyberbullying, as well as specific policies regarding the use of electronic devices like cell phones and digital recording devices. Chapter 3 discusses the need to address teacher off-campus speech via policy and provides a sample employee blogging policy. Chapter 4 discusses the need for policies that address student privacy and data security. Chapter 5 discusses filtering and the need for policies that describe the rights and responsibilities of students, teachers, and staff with regard to accessing inappropriate materials. Chapter 6 discusses copyright and the need for an updated copyright compliance policy. These are just a few examples of policies school leaders will be charged with drafting for their schools.

THE ROLE OF THE SCHOOLS

There are a number of things schools must do if they want the policies they draft to be effective. The first is that school leaders need to frankly acknowledge the legal risks in today's 21st century-classroom environment. Legal claims relating to school computer and Internet use can arise even in the absence of intentional wrongdoing. School leaders need to identify all the foreseeable risks to students, teachers, and staff and take reasonable precautions to minimize those risks.

Schools also need to establish and communicate clear boundaries to all members of the school community. Part of this communication is that the school Internet system exists for a limited educational purpose. Schools should emphasize that the school Internet system is primarily intended for students, class assignments, and staff professional-development activities.

As part of the communication effort, schools must be prepared to provide educational programming for students as well as professional-development training for teachers and staff regarding appropriate use of school computers and the school Internet system, student and Internet privacy issues, appropriate monitoring of student Internet use, and appropriate measures to take when issues or concerns arise. In fact, with regard to the third issue above, the school board's concerns about what the teacher may say in his stand-up comic routine may be resolved via education. The teacher very likely could make small adjustments to his stand-up comedy act that would alleviate the school board's concerns about student privacy and teacher off-duty speech without negatively affecting the quality of his act.

Schools should also establish a policy describing the recommended chain of command for reporting incidents. In tandem with this policy, schools may want to craft age-appropriate tests students must pass before being granted a "license" to participate in less-structured Internet activities, such as online chat rooms and social-networking sites.

Five-Step Plan for Drafting School Policy

1. *Collect data.* Review existing school policies and identify the gaps in those policies. Identify the objectives for the new/revised policy. Gather data from educational associations, publications, other schools, and legal sources relating to the new/revised policy.

2. *Solicit input.* Invite teachers, staff, parents, and other stakeholders to provide comments regarding the content and structure of the new/revised policy.

3. *Draft the new/revised policy.* Refer to your particular school's procedures to determine who will be charged with drafting and what procedures should be followed.

4. *Circulate the draft of the new/revised policy.* Solicit feedback from members of the school community.

5. *Approve and disseminate the new/revised policy.* Refer to your particular school's procedures to determine the necessary approval process. Disseminate the approved policy to parents and ensure that the new policy is included in print and hard-copy student handbooks. Communicate news of the approved policy to other members of the school community.

Finally, schools need to acknowledge their role in educating parents about computer and Internet issues. Schools need to communicate early and often with parents, beginning with fall mailings and open houses and continuing through the school year as events occur or new technology is incorporated. Schools must keep parents apprised of how students are using the Internet in the classroom. They also need to advise parents that, although the district monitors student use of the system at school, parents still need to discuss individual family values with children. Most important, schools need to obtain parent consent before allowing student use of the school's computer and Internet system.

Sample Policy Language: Parents' Responsibility

I. Outside of school, parents bear responsibility for the same guidance of Internet use as they exercise with information sources such as television, telephones, radio, movies, and other possibly offensive media. Parents are responsible for monitoring their student's use of the school district system and of the Internet if the student is accessing the school district system from home or a remote location.

II. Parents will be notified that their students will be using school district resources/accounts to access the Internet and that the school district will provide parents the option to request alternative activities not requiring Internet access. This notification should include:

   (a) A copy of the user notification form provided to the student user.
   (b) A description of parent/guardian responsibilities.
   (c) A notification that the parents have the option to request alternative educational activities not requiring Internet access and the material to exercise this option.
   (d) A statement that the Student Online Acceptable Use Consent Form must be signed by the user, the parent or guardian, and the supervising teacher prior to use by the student.
   (e) A statement that the school district's acceptable use policy is available for parental review.

Source: Internet Acceptable Use and Safety Policy (Policy 524), Edina Public Schools.

CONCLUSION

The flexibility of contract law makes it ideal for establishing the parameters of the school community. Contracts can take the form of any number of common school documents and can be customized to meet nearly any situation. Acceptable use policies are the most common kind of contract used by schools. Other contracts include student handbooks, photo releases, and permission forms. Schools should take care in drafting contracts by thoroughly researching their options, anticipating potential problems, soliciting input from members of the school community, and consulting legal counsel. Once finalized, school contracts should be revisited regularly.

Checklist Regarding Policies and Procedures

Has your district done the following?

☐ **Made an assessment of legal risks arising from use of classroom technology?** School leaders need to identify all the foreseeable risks to students, teachers, and staff arising from the uses of technology in its classrooms. This book gives an overview of the many issues schools may encounter. Schools should communicate with legal counsel with regard to their specific technology uses and practices to assess any legal implications. Policy contracts should be drafted to address any potential issues identified.

☐ **Communicated clear expectations and boundaries with regard to all uses of technology in the classroom?** It is important that users of school technology resources know that the resources are for limited educational purposes. Schools should emphasize that the school Internet system is primarily intended for students, class assignments, and staff professional-development activities.

☐ **Enlisted student, staff, and parent input in drafting school technology contracts?** Enlist school technology stakeholders in the review and drafting of technology contracts. Parent, student, teacher, and staff participation will more accurately define actual practices and generate greater acceptance of final policies.

☐ **Established training requirements and policy acceptance procedures prior to allowing use of technology resources?** It is important that schools obtain acknowledgment from students, parents, and staff that they have familiarized themselves with school expectations with regard to computer and Internet use and that they accept the terms and conditions of use as stated in school technology contracts. Schools may also establish training requirements regarding appropriate use of school technology resources prior to allowing users access to such resources.

☐ **Incorporated parent education into your school's technology strategy?** Schools should communicate their technology policies and expectations to parents at every opportunity. New school year mailings and open houses provide opportunities to apprise parents of school technology policies. Schools should also advise parents of the need to discuss their family's values and expectations with regard to Internet use inside and outside the school setting.

☐ **Established a chain of command for reporting incidents?** It is important that school technology-use policies have clear, simple procedures for reporting, monitoring, and resolving incidents involving potential violations of school technology contracts.

Online Resources

Acceptable Use Policies: A Handbook. Virginia Department of Education. Division of Technology.

http://www.doe.virginia.gov/VDOE/Technology/AUP/home.shtml

Acceptable Use Policies for Internet Use.

http://www.media-awareness.ca/english/resources/special_initiatives/wa_resources/wa_teachers/backgrounders/acceptable _use.cfm

Internet Acceptable Use Policy Guidelines.

http://www.education-world.com/a_curr/curr093.shtml

Internet Acceptable Use Policy Template, Mississippi State Auditor's Office.

http://www.osa.state.ms.us/downloads/iupg.pdf

Network Montana Project Internet Acceptable Use Policy Template.

http://www.auditnet.org/docs/internet_acceptable_use_policy_t.htm

Ethical Issues

Developing Responsible Internet Citizens

The information technology (IT) staff for the Boston public schools uses a software program that allows it to control and track the Internet use of the city's 70,000 users and 12,000 computers spread throughout the city's schools. On a particular day in the spring of 2006, the IT staff reported there were over 85,000 clicks on Web pages relating to shopping at eBay, Craigslist, and retail Web sites. The shopping took place during school hours and consumed large portions of the Boston schools' available Internet bandwidth, slowing access to educationally legitimate Web sites.

As of 2000, a corporation called Zap Me! had made inroads into approximately 9% of all U.S. secondary schools. Zap Me! offered middle schools and high schools "free" computers, Internet connections, printers, and access to educational Web sites in exchange for a promise by schools that students would use Zap Me! for a minimum of four hours each school day. Zap Me! computers displayed on-screen advertising and utilized tracking equipment. When students logged on to Zap Me! the system automatically collected the student's age, sex, and zip code.

Eight teenagers were arrested in Lakeland, Florida, for their brutal attack on a 16-year-old girl. The teens lured their victim to a friend's home for the sole purpose of video taping the attack and posting it on YouTube and MySpace. During the attack, which was described as animalistic, one of the teens struck the girl on the head several times and slammed her head into a wall, knocking her unconscious. A search of YouTube's video archive after the attack revealed dozens of clips depicting beatings and other violence inflicted by teens upon each other, some of which may have been staged for the camera.

U p to this point, this book has focused on the legal issues that can arise in schools equipped with technology. There are a number of them, for sure. As technology continues to evolve and more and more electronic devices make their way into the classroom, the law will evolve too. It will just take time.

The law is not the only thing that needs to catch up with technology, though. Technology presents a number of ethical issues for its users, and as a society, we have yet to decide on all the ethical ground rules for using computers and the Internet. The Internet, in particular, is problematic because of the anonymity it provides its users. The U.S. evangelist Dwight Lyman Moody is credited with the quote, "Character is what you are in the dark." What Moody means is that a person's true character comes out when others cannot see what the person is doing—when that person is "in the dark." For some, being able to e-mail, instant message, and post messages on blogs and Web sites, without having to identify themselves or physically witness the effect their messages have on the people the messages have been sent to, is a modern day version of operating in the dark. Some people make good decisions when sitting at their keyboards. Some do not.

CYBER ETHICS

Laws help us address the worst ills in society. There are, and should be, laws against stealing another person's identity, destroying another's reputation, electronically accessing another's bank account, luring a teenage girl to a meeting spot in the hopes of obtaining sex, and other similar acts. But what about conduct that does not rise to the level of criminality? What about behavior that is merely rude, upsetting, or unfair? If we are going to provide students with computers, Internet access, cell phones, and the like, we have an obligation to teach them how to use these tools ethically.

The three scenarios at the beginning of the chapter highlight the fact that all of us, regardless of age or status, are guilty of ethical breaches when it comes to the Internet. Some of these breaches are more serious than others. The first example above is perhaps the mildest. It involves inappropriate use of a school resource by a number of users: students, teachers, staff, and possibly even administrators. It is likely that no one user is spending hours shopping and tying up the school server. Rather, it is the totality of users that have caused the problem. The end result, though, is that a school resource designed to assist students and teachers in their educational endeavors is misused.

The second example offers a new twist on an old theme. Is it ethical for schools to allow commercial entities to access students in exchange for badly needed school resources? Schools have faced this dilemma for years. Many have agreed to give exclusive rights to soft-drink providers or to name school gymnasiums and theaters after corporate sponsors in exchange for funding or better facilities for their students. In the example above, though, there is an added component to this exchange. Students using the Zap Me! computers are not only subjected to advertising, they are unwittingly providing data to Zap Me! advertisers. Is this worth the *free* computer equipment?

The third example is, of course, the most troubling. The teens involved clearly are guilty of criminal acts, but they just as clearly lack good ethical decision-making skills. Mesmerized by the pop culture status of being featured on YouTube, they completely disregarded the effect their actions would have on their victim or even their own futures. As was discussed in Chapter 1, teens do not always think through their actions when using technology. Their lack of forethought and technology's ability to produce an immediate result can be a dangerous combination. If schools are going to provide students with computers and Internet access, ethics training must be provided as well.

ETHICS TRAINING

Ethics training is necessary for all computer and Internet users. The optimal time for introducing ethics training, though, is when children are first exposed to computers. As students learn to use school computers, teachers and staff can facilitate discussions about ethical behavior. Teachers can build ethical components into instruction, assignments, and assessments. They can help students build an awareness of their actions as well as an understanding that harmful acts committed in cyberspace really do hurt people. David Whittier (2006) makes this point very clearly in his article, *Cyberethics in the Googling Age:*

> Young people . . . need examples and stories that illustrate the harm of invading someone's privacy, stealing someone's personal information, stealing software or music or copying another's writing without attribution. They need to see how hate speech, cyber bullying, and rumor spreading hurt people. They need to see how invading someone's privacy online is a lack of respect—not only for others, but also for oneself. They can benefit from seeing how creating a false identity is associated with being untrustworthy and to understand what the consequences of not being trusted can be. They need to understand that responsible computing is the same thing as being responsible in the real world. They need to understand that hate speech, cyber bullying, and rumor spreading via technology are unjust and unfair and they would not want to be the recipients of unjust or unfair treatment. They need to understand that it takes courage to be an ethical user of Internet and other technologies, and to help others to do so (65).

Dr. Marvin Berkowitz, a behavioral development expert at St. Louis University has performed research on the topic of student ethics training. He recommends starting ethics training at the gateway age of 9 to 12 years, the same age at which other groups begin their message delivery (e.g., substance abuse and sex education). Berkowitz points out that 9 to 12 years old is the point in development where children begin to understand abstract values like privacy rights and can begin to evaluate the consequences of their actions (Berkowitz cited in Kruger, 2003).

In addition, the Cybercitizen Partnership, an educational organization with which Berkowitz is affiliated, advocates relating real-world behavior (entering a neighbor's house without permission) to cyber-world behavior (accessing someone else's computer without permission). It takes the position that, because most of the bad behavior occurring on the Internet can be tied to real-world incidents and teachers routinely teach real-world behavior, the transition to online actions should not be difficult for children to make (Smith, 2008).

The Office of Information Technology of the University of Virginia produced an award winning video in 2001 promoting responsible computing in a unique and paradoxical way. The video features various teens speaking to the camera. Each clip starts with a teen saying, "When I go to UVa, I want to . . ." then continues with a variety of responses, including the following:

- Open e-mail accounts and get a virus
- Post obscene messages on the Internet
- Commit fraud using someone else's identity
- Violate copyright laws
- Hack into government computer and go to federal prison

The video effectively drives home its message at its conclusion when it asks the question, "How much trouble can you buy with your computer?" The video may be viewed at http://www.itc.virginia.edu/pubs/docs/RespComp/videos/home.html.

There are a number of good sources of ethics training materials. One such source is the Cybercitizen Awareness Program. The program offers a variety of online resources at http://www.cybercitizenship.org/. The strategies endorsed by the program are simple and easily incorporated into the classroom setting: have a basic understanding of the technology being used and the options it offers, participate with students online, educate students about the standards that have been established for school computer use, and encourage parents to work with their students to create a set of "rules of the online road" that align with their household's expectations relating to both computer ethics and safety.

Cyber Ethics: Some Educator-Recommended Student Activities

- Interview adults and students about their views on responsible use of computing and safety online.
- Create posters, slideshows, and multimedia presentations focusing upon safe, legal, and moral uses of computers. Post the student creations in classrooms, in the computer lab and on your school's Web site.
- Hold mock trials in which students role-play lawyers, prosecutors, defendants, witnesses, and judges in cases dealing with irresponsible and illegal use of computers and the Internet.
- Research news stories about ethical and legal problems related to technology and then discuss the stories in class.
- Create a database of information about your students. Then have the teacher alter the information without the students knowing it. Have students use the altered database and see what they discover. A lively discussion should follow.
- Hold a responsible-computing panel discussion and invite parents and community leaders to participate.
- Write articles for local newspapers featuring information about what they are doing to solve ethical problems in using technology.

Source: Marsh, M. (1998). Piracy, pornography, plagiarism, propaganda, privacy: Teaching children to be responsible users of technology protects their rights and the rights of others. Computer Learning Foundation, http://www.computerlearning.org/articles/Ethics98.htm.

For schools to assume an active role in ethics training, schools also need to ensure that teachers and staff members have a good understanding of technology and the ethical issues it creates. Good staff development programs can provide a foundation. Teachers and staff members also need to share with each other what they are learning from students and what they are seeing in the classroom. For instance, a staff-development program that provides statistics about an increase in technology-assisted cheating among students will increase awareness among teachers that students are becoming more creative in their cheating methods, but the effectiveness of that program is increased when teachers who witness cheating firsthand—whether by the student who feeds his iPod earbud up his sleeve so he can rest his head on his shoulder during a history exam and listen to his prerecorded answers or by the student who brings a soft-drink bottle with a cleverly crafted label bearing key formulas to her chemistry test—share their experiences with other teachers and staff.

Ten Commandments of Computer Ethics

1. Thou shalt not use a computer to harm other people.

2. Thou shalt not interfere with other people's computer work.

3. Thou shalt not snoop around in other people's computer files.

4. Thou shalt not use a computer to steal.

5. Thou shalt not use a computer to bear false witness.

6. Thou shalt not copy or use proprietary software for which you have not paid.

7. Thou shalt not use other people's computer resources without authorization or proper compensation.

8. Thou shalt not appropriate other people's intellectual output.

9. Thou shalt think about the social consequences of the program you are writing or the system you are designing.

10. Thou shalt always use a computer in ways that insure consideration and respect for your fellow humans.

Source: Computer Ethics Institute, 11 Dupont Circle, NW Suite 900, Washington, DC 20036.

CONCLUSION

The ethical pitfalls associated with technology confronting today's students are numerous. They include cyberbullying; misrepresenting one's age or identity on social-networking sites, in chat rooms, or to access pornography; misrepresenting oneself or others by doctoring and posting digital photos; plagiarism and cheating (often with the assistance of electronic devices like cell phones and iPods); and overuse of the Internet to the extent that it affects one's social and physical well-being (sometimes referred to as Internet addiction). The list is likely to grow as new electronic devices become available. Technology offers students tempting alternatives. Schools must offer students the education and support they need to use technology ethically.

Checklist Regarding Ethical Issues

Has your district done the following?

☐ **Designed and instituted ethics training for all computer and Internet users?** Start ethics training for children at ages 9 to 12, when children understand abstract values like privacy rights and can evaluate the consequences of their actions. Analogize bad behavior on the Internet to similar real-world behaviors to illustrate consequences. Reinforce appropriate computer use with age-appropriate computer ethics training for older student technology users. Use teachers and staff-development programs to provide adult users with an understanding of technology and the ethical issues it creates.

Online Resources

Codes of Ethics Online: Computing and Information Systems, *Illinois Institute of Technology.*

http://ethics.iit.edu/codes/index_detailed.php?key=cis&PHPSESSID=2af 20582d2fac0b2814d4a1c24e2714b (multiple links from this site)

IJIRE: International Journal of Internet Research Ethics.

http://www.uwm.edu/Dept/SOIS/cipr/ijire

CHAPTER NINE

Looking Ahead

Keeping an Eye on the Future

As the introduction to this book states, technology has breathed new life into the classroom; technology has also raised a myriad of legal, ethical, and social issues for schools. Schools have been charged with a huge responsibility with regard to educating students in the 21st-century classroom. For that reason, schools should consider investing energy and resources in shaping the new laws that will govern them and their students.

How can schools shape new laws? They can research, draft, and enforce effective school policies—a contract law approach. They can educate students, staff, and teachers about issues involving liability, taking corrective measures when necessary to quell disputes and avoid harm—a case law approach. And they can work with municipal, state, and federal lawmakers to ensure that the codified law being enacted in response to technology issues is comprehensive and fair—a statutory law approach. It is this final approach that offers the most opportunity.

Schools can influence the subject matter and breadth of statutory law in a number of ways. When it comes to statutory law, timing is everything. Keeping tabs on proposed legislation and, more important, being active proponents of legislation they know will serve schools well put teachers and school leaders in the driver's seat.

One way schools keep tabs is by appointing legislative liaisons to track proposed and pending legislation on the state and national levels, inform the greater school community about that legislation, and identify opportunities to influence that legislation. Schools typically appoint liaisons at the district level and provide them with training, resources, and nominal release time to carry out their work.

Schools can also track legislation through state-education agencies and educational-trade associations. Associations are excellent sources of legislative information. In addition, associations typically provide lobbying services and have state or nationally based memberships, which allow them to rally others to action. Members of the school community can regularly visit legislative action center Web sites, such as those hosted by the National Education Association (NEA) and the American Association of School Administrators (AASA), for updates on education issues pending before Congress. Many associations also publish legislative news e-mail newsletters or **rich site summary (RSS) feeds** that deliver news about legislative developments as they arise.

On the state level, initiatives can be tracked using the National Conference of State Legislatures (NCSL) legislative tracking Web resources or via the Web sites for the separate state educational offices and agencies. A full listing of state education office and agency Web sites, many of which contain their own legislative news sections, is available through the U.S. Department of Education at http://wdcrob colp01.ed.gov/Programs/EROD/org_list.cfm?category_ID=SEA.

Legislative action does not have to be limited to the district liaison. Many schools with appointed liaisons find they benefit from encouraging other teachers and staff members to get involved legislatively too. Schools interested in generating interest and support among members of the school community in this regard should consider providing resources and release time so interested staff members can attend advocacy institutes, workshops, or training sessions, such as those sponsored by the American Library Association (ALA). Schools are also encouraged to include legislative research among the duties required of school legal counsel.

By making legislation a priority, schools ensure they will have a voice in the law-making process. When schools bring their experience and expertise to the legislative process, better laws result. It is at least in part because of the efforts of schools and the ALA that the highly criticized H.R. 5319 Deleting Online Predators Act (DOPA) was defeated. Teachers and librarians opposed DOPA because the language of the bill was overbroad, and there was a significant risk that students and library users in the poorest communities would be prevented from accessing appropriate content and from learning how best to safely manage their own Internet access. As was noted in Chapter 5, the legislation that has been proposed since DOPA does not pose this same risk and is much more school friendly.

CONCLUSION

Teachers, staff, and school administrators witness firsthand the effects of technology in the classroom. They are the ones in the trenches. They see how much technology can contribute to the educational experience, and they see the dark side of technology as well.

With all its advantages and disadvantages, one thing is certain: Technology is a part of 21st-century education. For that reason, schools must be proactive. Rather than sit back and let others dictate the rules regarding technology and education, schools should take action. Schools have much to add to the discussion, and they have a vested interest in shaping the laws that will govern them and their school communities into the future.

Checklist Regarding Keeping an Eye on the Future

Has your district done the following?

☐ **Implemented procedures for monitoring proposed legislation?** Many schools appoint legislative liaisons to track proposed and pending legislation on state and national levels. You should consider also requiring school legal counsel to provide periodic legislative updates. Education agencies and educational-trade associations are good resources for legislative information. Legislative news e-mails and RSS feeds deliver news about legislative developments as they arise.

☐ **Established methods for effective advocacy regarding legislation affecting schools?** How will your school respond to those pieces of legislation your district supports or opposes? Advocacy based on your school's expertise and experience will result in better, more effective laws.

Online Resources

Kansas National Education Association. Communicating With Legislators.
   http://ks.nea.org/legislative/rules.html

National School Boards Association Advocacy Action Plan.
   http://www.nsba.org/MainMenu/Advocacy/TalktoCongress.aspx

Resource A

How Laws Affect the Schools and Teachers
Who Embrace Technology in Learning

W hen discussing the specific legal issues that can arise in today's K–12 public-school environment, it is important to have an understanding of where laws come from and how laws affect schools. Generally speaking, there are three different types of law with which schools need to be familiar: (1) statutory law, (2) common law, and (3) contract law.

Statutory law is the law drafted by our state and federal lawmakers to address particular scenarios or prohibit particular activities. It often has a direct impact on school policy because it is crafted with a particular problem or goal in mind. For instance, several *statutes* have been drafted on the federal level to address issues of Internet filtering in public schools. These statutes govern public schools in all 50 states.

Common law is the law developed by courts on a case-by-case basis to handle specific disputes between parties. Common law is judge-made law. It indirectly shapes school policy because the decisions made by judges create *precedent*. Precedent means the decisions by a judge in one jurisdiction can influence judges in other jurisdictions. For instance, a decision by an Alaskan court about a student's free-speech rights, though based on a specific incident at an Alaskan school, might influence an Illinois court's ruling on a similar issue because there are relatively few student free-speech cases brought to court and the Alaskan decision would offer a current legal evaluation of and guidance on the issue. Accordingly, common law influences school districts as they make decisions about policies. Even if no legal decisions have been rendered in the state in which a school district resides, decisions from other states can serve as predictors of how similar legal disputes might be treated in the school district's own state and, accordingly, may affect that district's policy decisions.

Contract law is the private law developed by and between parties to address specific situations and relationships. We refer to it as private law because it can be customized to fit the needs of particular parties. Contracts are flexible, both in the sense that parties can use them to create their own rules of the game at the outset of their relationship and because parties can change those rules (i.e., can amend the terms of their contracts) if they agree that changing the rules makes sense in light of changing circumstances. Because of this flexibility, contract law is ideally suited to handling technology-related issues. In schools, contract law commonly takes the form of acceptable use policies, bullying policies, parent permission slips, photographic releases, and various other agreements involving students, parents, and schools.

Why is it important for teachers and school leaders to understand the different sources of law governing the school environment? Among other reasons, understanding the different sources of law can help teachers and school leaders determine where there is flexibility in school governance and where there is not and, as a result, what must be enforced in the staff room and the classroom versus what merely can be managed.

Statutory law, by and large, provides very little maneuverability. Schools must follow statutes strictly as written or risk the consequences (which often involve funding). One example of a statute that affects school policy is the Children's Internet Protection Act (CIPA). Signed into law in December 2000, CIPA created quite a stir among teachers and librarians because it requires libraries and schools to install filters on Internet computers to keep federal funding, including E-Rate discounts for computers and computer access. CIPA requires that Internet safety policies be adopted to monitor the Internet activity of minors and that Internet blocking or filtering devices be used to ensure material harmful to minors cannot be accessed through school and library computers. Under CIPA, school staff may disable filters for adults who are using school computers, if those adults are conducting bona fide research.

Because CIPA is a federal statute, it essentially acts as a mandate for all public schools. It is law that only can be changed by an act of Congress. That does not mean teachers and school leaders cannot take action to try to change the law. They can. But as recent efforts to change the No Child Left Behind statute demonstrate, trying to change statutes after they have become law is difficult.

With regard to common law, teachers and school leaders can turn to state education agencies and educational-trade associations for updates on pending legal cases and common law decisions. Tracking case law developments in their school districts' state of residence, as well as developments in other states, enables school leaders to enact preventative measures and "head off at the pass" legal disputes and actual lawsuits.

Contract law, the third type of law affecting schools, offers schools the greatest measure of control and flexibility. Whether negotiating the purchase of computers for the school mediacenter, determining the parameters of an Internet-based staff-development program, or entering into a collaborative agreement with a neighboring school district to offer online courses, contract law allows school leaders to incorporate their schools' values and priorities when creating the private law for their districts.

In summary, numerous types of laws affect the K–12 public-school environment. Because different laws affect schools differently, it is important to understand where different laws come from and the amount of flexibility allowed by those laws when applying them to the school setting. Teachers and school leaders need to familiarize themselves with school law. They also should consider whether they have a professional obligation to get politically involved in the passage or repeal of those laws by openly opposing harmful laws and supporting effective, well-crafted laws.

Resource B

Sample Acceptable Use Policy

[DISTRICT] ACCEPTABLE USE OF COMPUTERS, COMPUTER NETWORKS, AND INTERNET RESOURCES

A. Introduction

The use of [District] computers, computer network, and Internet resources is a key element of the curriculum and instruction in [District]. The [District] computer network is intended for educational purposes. [District] expects that staff will incorporate appropriate use of computer network and Internet resources into the curriculum and will provide guidance and instruction to students as to their uses.

Despite its tremendous educational potential, the Internet also presents the potential for security vulnerabilities and user abuse. For safety purposes, [District] employs both an Internet filter and firewall. [District] maintains compliance with the Children's Internet Protection Act (CIPA). The board expects all employees and students to abide by the [District] Acceptable Use of Computers, Computer Networks, and Internet Resources Procedures set forth below. Failure to follow the guidelines will result in disciplinary action. [District] is not responsible for ensuring the accuracy or usability of any information found on external networks.

Parent(s)/guardian(s) will be given the opportunity to determine their child's access to the Internet when they first begin school in [District], Grade 3, Grade 6, and Grade 9. [District] will not be responsible for any and all claims arising out of or related to the usage of this interconnected computer system.

B. Access

1. [District] offers Internet access for staff and student use. This policy sets forth the online acceptable use procedures for all staff and students using the district's computers and network. This acceptable use policy applies to all technologies capable of

accessing, inputting or extracting information/data from the district's computer network, electronic mail (e-mail), and Internet.

2. Students and employees shall have access to Internet World Wide Web information resources through their classroom, library, or school computer lab.

3. Students and their parent(s)/guardian(s) must sign an Acceptable Use Consent Form to be granted access to the Internet via the [District] computer network.

4. A signature will be required when they first begin school in [District], Grade 3, Grade 6, and Grade 9. Parent(s)/guardian (s) can withdraw their approval at any time.

5. The school district shall provide each employee, where appropriate, an e-mail account.

6. Students shall be provided limited educational access to a classroom/library e-mail account upon request of their classroom teacher for completion of curriculum-related assignments.

7. The use of the school district system and access to use of the Internet is a privilege, not a right. The school district reserves the right to limit or remove any user's access to the school district's computer system, equipment, e-mail system, and Internet access at any time for any reason. Depending on the nature and degree of the violation and the number of previous violations, unacceptable use of the school district system or the Internet may result in one or more of the following consequences: suspension or cancellation of use or access privileges; payments for damages and repairs; loss of credit and/or reduction of grade; discipline under other appropriate school district policies, including suspension, expulsion, exclusion, or termination of employment; or civil or criminal liability under other applicable laws.

C. Educational Purpose

1. The [District] computer network has not been established as a public access service and is not an "open" or "limited open" forum. The term "educational purposes" includes, but is not limited to, information management, classroom activities, media-center projects, educational research, career development, and curriculum activities using computers and Internet resources.

2. The [District] computer network has not been established as a public access service or a public forum. [District] has the right to

place reasonable restrictions on the material accessed or posted through the system into the intranet, e-mail, Web sites, and list server. Students and employees are expected to follow the rules set forth in this policy and the law when using the [District] computer network. The network will be monitored by staff to ensure educational utilization.

3. Students and employees may not use the [District] computer network for noneducational commercial purposes. This means that no products or services may be offered, provided, or purchased through the [District] computer network, unless such products or services are for a defined educational purpose and such activity has been preapproved by [District].

4. The [District] computers may not be used for political lobbying. It may be used to communicate with elected representatives and to express opinions to them on political issues.

D. Your Rights and Responsibilities

1. Free Speech

   Student right to free speech is set forth [District Policy], which applies also to communication on the Internet. The [District] computer network is considered a limited forum, similar to the school newspaper, and, therefore, the district may restrict speech for valid educational reasons. The district shall not restrict speech on the basis of a disagreement with the opinions expressed.

2. Search and Seizure

   a. Students and employees should not expect any privacy in the contents of personal files on the district system. Administrators and faculty may review files and messages to maintain system integrity and ensure that users are acting responsibly.

   b. The district may examine all information stored on district technology resources at any time. The district may monitor staff and student technology usage. Electronic communications, all data stored on the district's technology resources, and downloaded material, including files deleted from a user's account, may be intercepted, accessed, or searched by a district administrator or designees at any time.

   c. Routine maintenance and monitoring of [District] computer system may lead to discovery that this policy or the following policies or laws have been violated: school board policy dealing with student conduct and district discipline, school board policy dealing with student civil and legal rights and responsibilities, board policy on staff activities, and/or federal, state, or local laws.

d. An individual search shall be conducted if there is reasonable suspicion that this policy, school board policies, and/or the law have been violated. The investigation shall be reasonable and related to the suspected violation.

e. Parent(s)/guardian(s) of students have the right at any time to request to see the contents of student's e-mail files.

3. District Employees

Rights, responsibilities, and duties of district employees as they relate to e-mail and Internet use are governed by the [District] Board of Education Policies and Procedures and the master agreements between the district and the employee bargaining units. Employees may be disciplined or terminated for violating the district's policies, regulations, and procedures.

4. Due Process

a. The district shall cooperate fully with local, state, or federal officials in any investigation related to any illegal activities conducted through [District] computer network.

b. In the event there is a claim that employees or students have violated this policy or other Board policy in use of the [District] computer network, they shall be provided with a written notice of the suspected violation and an opportunity to present an explanation as defined in school board policy for students and bargaining agreements for staff.

c. If the violation also involves a violation of other provisions of school board policy, it shall be handled in a manner described in school board policy which deals with dismissal, including suspension, exclusion, and expulsion. Additional restrictions may be placed on use of individual Internet accounts, or could result in suspension, expulsion, and/or financial liability.

E. Unacceptable Uses

The following uses of the [District] computer network are considered unacceptable:

1. Personal Safety

a. Students and employees shall not post or provide personal contact information about themselves or other people on the Internet. Personal contact information includes a student's or employee's home address or telephone number, a student's school address, and an employee's work address. It is not a violation of this policy to include the school's return address on outgoing e-mail communications.

b. Students shall not agree to meet with someone contacted or met online without parent's approval. Parent(s)/guardian(s) should accompany students to approved meetings.

c. Students shall promptly disclose to their teacher or other school employee any message received that is inappropriate or causes discomfort.

2. Illegal Activities

a. Students and employees shall not attempt to gain unauthorized access to [District] computer network or to any other computer system through [District] computer network or go beyond authorized access. This includes attempting to log in through another person's account or access another person's files. These actions are illegal, even if only for the purposes of "browsing."

b. Students and employees shall not make deliberate attempts to disrupt the computer system or destroy data by spreading computer viruses or by any other means. These actions are illegal, and criminal prosecution and/or disciplinary action will be pursued.

c. Students and employees shall not use the [District] computer network system to engage in any act that is illegal; that facilitates gambling; or that violates any local, state, or federal statute.

d. Students and staff shall not use the Internet or the district's computer network to harass or threaten the safety of others.

e. Misuse of the computer equipment or network including, but not limited to, deletion or violation of password protected information, computer programs, data, password or system files; inappropriate access of files, directories, Internet sites; deliberate contamination of system, unethical use of information, or violation of copyright laws is prohibited.

3. System Security

a. Employees are responsible for their individual e-mail accounts and should take all reasonable precautions to prevent others from being able to use their accounts. Under no condition should staff provide their login identity and/or passwords to another person.

b. Students shall immediately notify a teacher or the system administrator if they have identified a possible security problem.

Students should not look for security problems, because this may be construed as an illegal attempt to gain access. Under no conditions should students provide other students with their login identity and/or network password.

c. Students and employees shall avoid the inadvertent spread of computer viruses by following the district virus protection procedures when downloading software or bringing disks into the school.

d. Students who gain access to teacher computer files, directory, programs, and Web site without permission from a teacher will be disciplined as defined in the student handbook.

e. The district will assign specific staff with security, management, and account responsibilities associated with the district's Internet resources and network accounts.

f. Tampering with the district's computer security system, and/or applications, and/or documents, and/or equipment, will be considered vandalism, destruction, and defacement of school property. Please be advised that it is a federal offense (felony) to break into any security system. Financial and legal consequences of such actions are the responsibility of the user and/or student's parent or guardian.

4. Inappropriate Language

a Restrictions against inappropriate language apply to public messages, private messages, and material posted on Web pages.

b. Students and employees shall not use obscene, profane, lewd, vulgar, rude, inflammatory, threatening, or disrespectful language.

c. Students and employees shall not post information that could cause damage or a danger of disruption.

d. Students and employees shall not engage in personal attacks, including prejudicial or discriminatory attacks, based on a person's race, gender, sexual orientation, religion, national origin, or disability, or engage in any other harassment or discrimination prohibited by school district policy or by law.

e. Students and employees shall not harass another person. Harassment is persistently acting in a manner that distresses or annoys another person. If students or staff are told by a person to stop sending them messages, they must stop.

f. Students and employees shall not knowingly or recklessly post false or defamatory information about a person or organization.

5. Respect for Privacy

   a. Students and employees shall not repost a message that was sent to them privately without permission of the person who sent them the message.

   b. Students and employees shall not post private information about another person on the Internet. This does not prohibit staff from discussing private student information with each other or with a student's parent or guardian via e-mail, in conformance with the Data Practices Act [cite], Student Privacy Act [cite], and applicable school district policies.

6. Respecting Resource Limits

   a. Students and employees shall use the system only for educational and career development activities and limited, high-quality self-discovery and [District] curriculum activities.

   b. Students and employees will have access to limited space on their school's computer server. Student ability to download files shall be limited by mediacenter and school policy. Users are responsible for making backup copies of the documents and files that are critical to their use.

   c. Students and employees shall not post chain letters or engage in spamming. (Spamming is sending an annoying or unnecessary message to a large number of people.)

   d. Students shall not deliberately or knowingly delete another student's or employee's file.

   e. Students and employees shall only use software, including but not limited to e-mail applications and Web browsers, that is supplied by the school district. Employees and students shall not install hardware or software on the school district's computer system without express permission of the director of media and technology services.

7. Plagiarism and Copyright Infringement

   a. Students and employees shall not plagiarize works that are found on the Internet. Plagiarism is taking the ideas or writings of others and presenting them as if they were yours.

   b. Students and employees shall respect the rights of copyright owners. Copyright infringement occurs when one inappropriately reproduces a work that is protected by a copyright. If a work contains language that specifies appropriate use of that work, follow the expressed requirements. If unsure whether or not work can be used, request permission from the copyright owner. Copyright law can be very confusing; ask media specialists for guidance as needed.

8. Inappropriate Access to Material

   a. Students and employees shall not use the [District] computer network to access material that is profane or obscene (pornography), contains viruses, network hacking programs, or similar programs that advocate illegal acts, or that advocates violence or discrimination towards other people (hate literature).

   b. If students mistakenly access inappropriate information, they should immediately tell their teacher, media specialist, or another district employee. This will protect them against claims that they have intentionally violated this policy.

   c. Parent(s)/guardian(s) should instruct students if there is additional material that they think it would be inappropriate for them to access. The district fully expects that students shall follow their parent's instructions in this matter.

   d. Educators will monitor student use of the Internet in schools and will take reasonable measures to prevent access by students to inappropriate materials on the Internet and World Wide Web and restrict access to materials harmful to students.

   e. The district will monitor the online activities of employees and students, and operate technology protection measures (filtering/blocking devices or software) on all computers on the district's computer network as required by law. The filtering/blocking software will attempt to protect against access to visual depictions that are obscene, harmful to students, and child pornography, as required by law. Invasion or disabling of the filtering/blocking device installed by the district, including attempts to evade or disable, is a violation of the acceptable use policy.

F. Limitation of Liability

The school district does not assume and, hereby, expressly disclaims liability for the misuse of its computers, equipment, e-mail, and Internet programs that violate this policy or any applicable law. The district makes no guarantee that the functions or the services provided by or through the district system shall be error-free or without defect. The district is not responsible for any damage suffered through the use of its computer system, including but not limited to, the loss of data, interruptions in service, the accuracy or quality of information obtained through or stored in the system, damages or injuries from improper communications, damage to property used to access school district computers or online resources, or financial obligations resulting from the use of school district resources.

Student Online Acceptable Use Consent Form

Each student is required to complete and sign a form that demonstrates his or her understanding of the school district's Student Online Acceptable Use. Students will receive directions at the beginning of the school year regarding how to ensure they have appropriate clearance to use the district's technology resources.

Student

By signing below I agree to follow the [District] Online Acceptable Use Procedures for technology as attached. I understand that my use of the network is a privilege and requires proper online etiquette. I further understand that misuse of the network shall result in disciplinary action.

Print Student Name: _____

Student's I.D. Number: _____

Student's Signature: _____

Address and Zip Code: _____

_____

_____

Telephone Number: _____

School Building: _____

Parent or Guardian

I give my permission for my child to have access to the Internet using the district's computer network. I also understand that some material accessible through the interconnected systems may be inappropriate for school-aged pupils. I agree to defend, indemnify, and hold harmless the [District] from any and all claims arising out of or related to the usage of this interconnected computer system. I further understand that I have the right to withdraw my approval at anytime.

Approved _____

Disapproved _____

Print Parent or Guardian's Name: _____

Signature of Parent or Guardian: _____

Date: _____

Glossary of Terms

Biometric identification tools: Tools that capture unique body characteristics for the purpose of identification and access (e.g., fingerprint readers).

The Children's Internet Protection Act (CIPA): A federal law that includes a mandate that public schools install filtering software in order to be eligible to receive federal E-Rate funding.

Copyright: A federal law that grants the creators of original works the exclusive right to reproduce, adapt, distribute, perform, and display their works.

Copyright infringement: The unauthorized or unlicensed use of a copyright-protected work.

Common law: The law developed by courts on a case-by-case basis to handle specific disputes between parties (also known as case law).

Contract law: The private law developed by and between parties to address specific situations and relationships.

Creative Commons: An organization that has developed an icon-based licensing scheme for use by copyright owners who wish to convey to potential users of copyrighted works how and to what extent those users may use the copyrighted work without specific permission.

Cyberbullying: The intentional and repeated harassment, humiliation, embarrassment, or harm of others through the use of computers, cell phones, and other electronic devices.

Digital divide: The gap between people with effective access to computers, the Internet, and information technology and those without effective access.

E-Rate: The common name for the Schools and Libraries Program of the Universal Service Fund that provides discounts to telecommunications carriers for delivering affordable services to various categories of customers, including schools and libraries.

The Family Educational Rights and Privacy Act (FERPA) of 1974 : A federal law governing the privacy of student records and the obligations of schools, primarily with regard to records access, retention, and disclosure.

Filtering software: Software that prevents access to particular Internet Web sites when the content of such Web sites is deemed to be inappropriate (e.g., obscene, pornographic, or otherwise harmful to minors) for the users of the computers on which the software is installed.

First Amendment: Part of the U.S. Constitution's Bill of Rights. The First Amendment protects citizens' freedoms of speech and religion, freedom of the press, freedom to peaceably assemble, and freedom to petition the government for redress of grievances.

Free speech: One of the protected rights set forth in the First Amendment to the U.S. Constitution. Free speech may be defined as the right to express any opinion in public, and the related right to hear the expressions of others, without censorship or restraint by the government.

Internet: A global system of interconnected computer networks that allow the interchange data and information.

Learning object repository: An online database or repository of educational materials and learning content.

Liability: Legal responsibility or obligation of one party to another arising by law, usually to compensate financially.

Limited forum: A place for expressive activity, but which may be subject to reasonable, content-neutral time, place, and manner restrictions; for example a school computer network or Internet system.

OpenCourseWare: A free and open digital publication of educational materials, organized as courses.

Public domain: Writings or other expressions that are not owned or controlled by anyone or subject to copyright or intellectual property law. Materials in the public domain are free and available for anyone to use for any purpose.

Public forum: A place for expressive activity. Examples of traditional public forums include public parks, street corners, and town squares.

Rich site summary (RSS) feed: A type of data file used to publish frequently updated works such as blog entries, news headlines, and podcasts in a standardized format.

Social-Networking site: A Web-based online community of people who share common interests and/or activities (i.e., Facebook or MySpace).

Statute: Written law; typically a legislative act that has been approved by the legislature and signed into law by the governing executive (i.e., a governor or president).

Statutory law: The law drafted by our state and federal lawmakers to address particular scenarios or prohibit particular activities.

Strong passwords: Passwords that are difficult for both humans and computer programs to detect because they consist of at least six characters; the characters are a combination of letters, numbers, and symbols that are typically case sensitive; and they do not contain common words or parts of the user's own name.

YouTube: A Web site that allows users to post and/or view video content.

Zero-tolerance policy: A rule or policy that sets forth prescribed penalties for violations that do not vary based on circumstances (e.g., age, intent, and number or severity of violations).

References

Ashmore, R. W. (2006). Blocking 'MySpace' from your space. *School Administrator, 63*(9), 7.

Ashmore, R. W., & Herman, B. M. (2006, May). Abuse in cyberspace. *School Administrator, 63*(5), 31–36.

Baldas, T. (2007, December 10). As "cyber-bullying" grows, so do lawsuits. *National Law Journal.* Retrieved February 1, 2008, from http://www.law .com/jsp/article.jsp?id=1197281074941.

Bethel School Dist. 403 v. Fraser, 478 U.S. 675 (1986).

Children's Internet Protection Act, 20 U.S.C. §6301 (2000).

Children's Online Privacy Act of 1998, 15 U.S.C. §§6501-6506 (1999).

Connick v. Myers, 461 U.S. 138 (1983).

Deleting Online Predators Act of 2006 (DOPA), H.R. 5319.

Dickerson, D. (2005). Cyberbullies on campus. *The University of Toledo Law Review, 37*(1).

Doninger v. Niehoff, No. 07–3885 (2d Cir. May 29, 2008).

Dwyer v. Oceanport School District et al., No. 03–6005 (D.N.J. filed March 31, 2005).

Family Educational Rights and Privacy Act of 1974 (FERPA), 20 U.S.C. §1232g; 34 CFR Part 99.

First, P. F., & Hart, Y. Y. (2002, October). Access to cyberspace: The new issue in educational justice. *Journal of Law and Education, 31*(4), 385–411.

Goldmann, H. (2007–2008, December/January). Reframing the debate. *Learning and Leading with Technology.* Retrieved November 12, 2008, from http://www .iste.org/Content/NavigationMenu/Publications/LL/LLIssues/Volume_35 _2007_2008_/DecemberJanuaryNo4/35446g.pdf.

Hazelwood School District v. Kuhlmeier, 484 U.S. 260 (1988).

Kruger, B. (2003). Talking to students about cyber-ethics. *TechLearning.* Retrieved November 12, 2008, from http://www.techlearning.com/ shared/printableArticle.php?articleID=15000129.

Marsh, M. (1998). *Piracy, pornography, plagiarism, propaganda, privacy: Teaching children to be responsible users of technology protects their rights and the rights of others.* Retrieved May 26, 2008, from, http://www.computerlearning .org/articles/Ethics98.htm.

Moody, D. (n.d.). *Bartlett's Quotations Online.* Retrieved February 2, 2008, from http://www.bartleby.com/73/187.html.

Morse v. Frederick, 551 U.S. ____, 127 S. Ct. 2618 (U.S. 2007).

Nitzschke, B. S. (2006, June). Investigating staff misuse of district technology. *School Administrator, 63*(6), 8.

Pickering v. Board of Education, 391 U.S. 563 (1968).

Protecting Children in the 21st Century Act, S49 (2007).

Rice, H. (2008, May 21). Students' phones seized over girls' nude photos: "It's child pornography," superintendent says. *The Houston Chronicle.* Retrieved May 22, 2008, from http://74.125.45.104/search?q=cache:XbGZkblrxYoJ :njbullying.org/documents/Houstoncyberarticle5-21-8.doc+houston+ chronicle+phones+seized+may+2008&hl=en&ct=clnk&cd=3&gl=us.

Shariff, S., & Johnny, L. (2007, March). Cyber-libel and cyber-bullying: Can schools protect student reputations and free-expression in virtual environments? *Education Law Journal, 16*(3), 301–342.

Smith, P. (2008). The cybercitizen partnership: Teaching children cyber ethics. *Cybercitizen Partnership.* Retrieved May 27, 2008, from http://cybercitizen ship.org/ethics/whitepaper.html.

Snyder v. Millersville University, et al., No. 2:2007cv01660 (E. D. Pa 2008).

Willard, N. (2000). Legal and ethical issues related to the use of the Internet in K–12 schools. *Brigham Young University Education & Law Journal, 2,* 225.

Willard, N. (2005). An educator's guide to cyberbullying and cyberthreats: Responding to the challenge of online social aggression, threats, and distress. *Center for Safe and Responsible Use of the Internet.* Retrieved May 25, 2008, from http://csriu.org/cyberbully/docs/cbcteducator.pdf.

Whittier, David. (2006). Cyberethics in the Googling age. *Journal of Education, 187*(2), 1–86.

Suggested Readings

Borja, R. (2006, October 11). Social-networking sites for schools promote safety, education benefits. *Education Week, 26*(7), 7.

Egelko, B. (2007, May 14). "Honk for peace" case tests limits on free speech. *San Francisco Chronicle,* p. A1.

Flowers, B. F., & Rakes, G. C. (2000). Analyses of acceptable use policies regarding the Internet in selected K–12 schools. *Journal of Research on Computing in Education, 32*(3), 351–365.

Illinois district leader suspended over gag video posted on Internet (2006, October 11). *Education Week, 26*(7), 6.

Hirsch, J. (2006, May). Is student blogging the new social disease? *The School Administrator, 63*(5), 8.

Jo, S. H. (2002, October).The legal standard on scope of teachers' free speech rights in the school setting. *Journal of Law and Education, 31*(4), 413.

Johnson, K., & Groneman, N. (2003). Legal and illegal use of the Internet: Implications for educators. *Journal of Education for Business, 78*(3), 147–152.

Kindred, K. A. (2006, February). The teacher in dissent: Freedom of expression in the classroom. *Education Law Journal, 15*(3), 207–231.

McClain, D. (2008, July 8). Internet program teaches harms of bullying to elementary students. *Milwaukee Journal Sentinel.* Available from http://www.jsonline.com/story/index.aspx?id=769920.

McMurtry, K. (2001, November). E-cheating: Combating a 21st century challenge. *T.H.E. Journal, 29*(4), 36–41.

Morgan, J., & VanLengen, C. (2005). The digital divide and K–12 student computer use. *Issues in Informing Science and Information Technology.* Available from http://proceedings.informingscience.org/InSITE2005/I56f86Morg.pdf.

Nitzschke, B. S. (2006, June). Investigating staff misuse of district technology. *School Administrator, 63*(6), 8.

Randel, D. (2007). *Bullying our kids in our homes: Welcome to cyber bullying.* Available from www.stoppingschoolviolence.com.

Richardson, W. (2006). *Blogs, wikis, podcasts, and other powerful Web tools for classrooms.* Thousand Oaks, CA: Corwin Press.

7 things you should know about Creative Commons. (2007, March). *EDUCAUSE Learning Initiative.* Available from http://www.educause.edu/Library Detail Page/666?ID=ELI7023.

Sleeper, L. (2006, March 1). Technology management: New tools make AUP enforcement easier than ever. *eSchool News Online.* Retrieved August 27, 2007, from http://www.eschoolnews.com.

Smith, M., & Blanchard, C. (2008, January 9). Facebook photos land Eden Prairie kids in trouble: More than 100 were suspended from activities or reprimanded after being shown drinking at parties. *The Star Tribune.* Retrieved January 15, 2008, from http://www.startribune.com/local/west/13549646.html.

Stansbury, M. (2007, August). Teachers gain tech skills while in their PJs: Home-based professional development is big success for Louisiana school district. *eSchool News online.* Retrieved August 27, 2007, from http://www.eschool-news.com.

Index

CORWIN
A SAGE Company

The Corwin logo—a raven striding across an open book—represents the union of courage and learning. Corwin is committed to improving education for all learners by publishing books and other professional development resources for those serving the field of PreK–12 education. By providing practical, hands-on materials, Corwin continues to carry out the promise of its motto: **"Helping Educators Do Their Work Better."**

War and Conflict

What's That Got To Do With Me?

War and Conflict

Antony Lishak

A+

Smart Apple Media

This book has been published in cooperation
with Franklin Watts.

Series editor: Adrian Cole, Design: Thomas Keenes,
Art director: Jonathan Hair, Picture researcher: Diana Morris

Acknowledgements:
Lynsey Addario/Corbis: 8, 28cl, 32. Martin Adler/Panos: 6cl,
18. Sally & Richard Greenhill/Alamy: 26. David
Grossman/Image Works/Topham: 6c, 11. Atef
Hassan/Reuters/Corbis: 2, 7, 31. Manchester Evening
News: 14. Jeff Paterson: 10. Photofusion/Alamy: front
cover t, back cover t, 27 (posed by models). Jason
Reed/Reuters/Corbis: front cover b, back cover b, 2-3, 19,
29. Rex Features: 9, 24. Alex Segre/Rex Features: 6cr, 13.
Courtesy of Sakue Shimohira and Nagasaki Foundation for
the Promotion of Peace: 20, 28c. Sipa Press/Rex Features:
21, 23, 25, 30. Topham: 15, 17. U.S. Pacifist Party: 22.

Published in the United States by Smart Apple Media
2140 Howard Drive West, North Mankato, Minnesota 56003

Library of Congress Cataloging-in-Publication Data

Lishak, Antony.
War and conflict / by Antony Lishak.
p. cm. — (What's that got to do with me?)
Includes index.
ISBN-13: 978-1-59920-039-2
1. War. 2. War and society. 3. Interpersonal conflict. I. Title.

U21.2.L525 2007
303.6'6—dc22   2006029892

9 8 7 6 5 4 3 2 1

Contents

So what?

Imagine a world in which war and conflict do not exist. You can't, can you? The sad fact is that ever since stone-age men clashed over who should have the biggest cave, disagreement has been part of our lives. Today, there is little sign that things are going to change.

What's it all about?

The closest most of us get to armed conflict is when we watch a film. But in the larger world, disputes between governments frequently result in sending soldiers into battle. In this book, you will meet a selection of people whose lives have been touched by war —a United States Marine, the survivor of an atomic bomb, and a child soldier. You will also read about everyday conflicts from a victim of bullying and a fan of war computer games.

Personal accounts

All of the testimonies are true. Some are first-hand accounts, while others are the result of bringing similar experiences together to create a single "voice." Every effort has been made to ensure they are authentic. To protect identities, a few names have been changed and models have posed for some of the pictures. Wherever possible, permission to use the information has been obtained.

Ask yourself

The testimonies won't tell you all there is to know about war and conflict; that wouldn't be possible. Instead, as you encounter the different views, think about your own opinions and experiences. This will help you begin to address the question: "War and conflict —what's that got to do with me?"

For many people, such as the Iraqis, armed conflict is part of their everyday lives.

A soldier

Thousands of soldiers choose to put their lives at risk in wars. Here, Major Tom Fisher explains why he is one of them.

I joined the U.S. Army 14 years ago to help others. That's why I'm here in Iraq—so that these people can be free. And it's not all fighting. Success here is measured by the millions of people who have clean drinking water and how many schools are constructed. War is not just one big shoot-'em-up computer game. It's all about back-up and support. This is what the military calls "logistics." There is a whole network of people working as one big

Soldiers are professional; they are specially trained for battle.

team—supporting each other. You know, over 5 million meals are served to the troops in a single week!

But I don't want you to think it's a vacation out here. People die in war—it can't be avoided. I've seen things that keep me awake at night, but my training helps me cope.

Fact bank

■ During the last 3,400 years, only 268 have been completely warless.

■ More than 108 million soldiers were killed in war and conflict during the 20th century.

■ In the 1990s alone, wars were responsible for the deaths of about 6.3 million civilians.

Flag-covered coffins of dead U.S. soldiers.

If someone wants to shoot me, he has to expect me to stop him.

And it's true, sometimes the wrong people get killed; war has always been messy. However, in today's world, war is necessary. Sad but true. To me it's about good and bad, right and wrong. I believe I am on the right side.

Ask yourself this . . .

■ Do you agree with Major Fisher? Can war be right? Is there a right side and wrong side in a conflict?

■ What causes, or people, would you be prepared to fight for?

A conscientious objector

Conscientious objectors are people who feel it is wrong to fight. Sometimes soldiers, when confronted with the reality of war, realize that they just could not kill. This is one such soldier.

My name is Stephen Funk. When I was 19, I enlisted as a U.S. Marine Corps reservist to serve in Iraq. I wasn't planning to join the military, but an army recruiter convinced me that basic training would give me a sense of direction in my life.

Stephen Funk spoke out against war, even though he had enlisted.

I soon discovered that the purpose of military training is to churn out non-thinking machines. I believe all humans have a natural aversion to killing and being forced to shout out "Kill! Kill! Kill!" every day damaged my mind, body, and soul. My revulsion toward violence grew stronger, but I was afraid to speak out. Then an instructor told me that I would be too weak to kill in a war situation. His goal was to toughen me up, but without thinking I replied that he was right. It was like breathing out after holding it in for two months.

From then on, I could not remain silent. I wanted others who may be thinking about enlisting to learn from my experiences. So I spoke out in public against the war. At first, some people told me I was a traitor and a coward— I even had a few death threats. However, I also received tremendous support, even from other enlisted men and women.

Anti-war protesters. Some people felt troops should not be sent to Iraq.

Fact bank

■ In March 2003, a U.S.-led force of around 170,000 troops invaded Iraq. Following a long dispute, they believed that the Iraqi president, Saddam Hussein, was developing weapons of mass destruction. About 50 U.S. reservists, like Stephen Funk, objected to the invasion. Stephen Funk was found guilty of desertion and spent five months in a military prison.

Ask yourself this . . .

■ What could the Marine Corps do to prevent people like Stephen Funk from joining in the first place?

■ When have you ever refused to do something because you felt it was wrong?

■ Who do you think deserves to be called a hero—Major Tom Fisher or Stephen Funk?

A computer games fan

Sam spends a lot of his life in war zones—through video games. Scientists disagree on how much people are affected by what they play, or if they are affected at all.

I'm fourteen and I love computer games. And let me tell you, there's more chance of a duck-billed platypus becoming president than there is of me becoming a crazed killer. It's just a game! If someone can't tell the difference between real life and fantasy, the problem's in their head, not on the screen.

In one game, I get points for *not* killing people, but helping them.

Sam sees a clear difference between real life and fantasy.

Fact bank

■ Some researchers believe war games that involve cooperation and teamwork between players could develop interpersonal skills. Other studies have shown that violent computer games help children to channel their aggression in a safe way. However, biological research has found that playing a computer game for a long time causes chemical changes in the human brain similar to those associated with taking illegal drugs.

The same sense of what's right and wrong that stops me from being violent in the real world affects the way I play computer games.

Anyway, all of these games come with safety guidelines and are rated, so parents can see if they are suitable for their children. If a four-year-old has nightmares because he has seen someone's brains blown out in an M-rated game, then it's the parents' fault!

Violent computer games, such as the one being played here, are often blamed for an increase in violent child behavior.

Ask yourself this . . .

■ To what extent do you think that the games Sam plays on his computer are likely to make him a more violent person?

■ Why aren't young children allowed to play whatever they want on a computer, for as long as they want?

■ When have you been stopped from buying or playing a computer game because someone thought it wasn't "suitable?"

A war veteran

What happens to soldiers when the fighting stops?
Here is the story of an Argentine war veteran who
served during the Falklands War in 1982. It seems
that once war is over, enemies can become friends.

My name is Alejandro Videla—I was
19 years old when I was sent to fight
against the British in the Malvinas
(the Falkland Islands). We were badly
equipped and didn't stand a chance.
We eventually surrendered to the
British troops. As prisoners of

war, we were given hot food and
clean clothes. We were just glad to be
alive and desperate to go home.

After the cease-fire, one of my
comrades accidentally set off a bomb
and was injured. Immediately, some

Alejandro Videla (left) with a British Falklands veteran on his visit to the United Kingdom (U

Fact bank

■ In 1982, Argentine armed forces invaded the Falklands, a small group of British-governed islands. The UK sent their armed forces in response, resulting in a conflict that lasted 72 days and claimed about 1,000 lives. Argentina still lays claim to the islands they call the Malvinas, although the two nations are now at peace.

Discarded Argentine equipment after the war.

British soldiers came and took him to the field hospital. His life was saved by the same men who, earlier, were trying to kill him.

But life back in Argentina was hard. I had to stop watching soccer because the giant fireworks set off by the crowd reminded me of the explosives. Many of my friends felt the same, but we were not allowed to ask for help. The government did not allow us to talk about the war in public.

Then I found a Web site for British war veterans and posted a question on the message board. I was contacted by one of the soldiers who helped my friend. He was finding life after the war difficult, too—at last we had someone to talk to who understood what we were both going through. When I came to visit him and his family in England, it was like finding a long-lost brother.

Ask yourself this . . .

■ Why do you think it helped Alejandro to contact a British war veteran?

■ How do you "make up" and trust someone again after you've had an argument?

■ Why do people forgive and forget?

Wartime technology

Some everyday things that we take for granted owe their existence, in part, to developments made during wartime. You just have to know what to look for, as this doctor has discovered.

My name is Dr. Adrian Richardson and I have to admit, although I don't like it, that many aspects of my work and life have directly benefited from war. Penicillin, the medicine that attacks dangerous bacteria in our bodies, was successfully developed during World War II (1939–45). I'm certain that the way car accident victims are treated today is because of the experiences of countless battlefield surgeons. The same is true for the treatment of burns and the use of plastic surgery.

Dr. Richardson believes there are some benefits to war.

All around my house are inventions that partly owe their existence to war. There's the microwave oven in the kitchen, the computer in my office and the smoke detectors in the hall. Then there are the satellites that tell us the weather and form the network connections for the Internet and cell phones. Also, my trip to Japan last year would never have been possible without wartime [jet] research. Yes, like it or not, without war the world would certainly be a different place.

Ask yourself this . . .

■ Which of the items that Dr. Richardson mentions would you find it most hard to live without?

■ How much do you agree that war is a good thing because of all the wartime medical advances outlined by the doctor?

Sir Frank Whittle and his jet engine.

Fact bank

■ The medicine penicillin was first discovered by Alexander Fleming in the early 1920s. Howard Florey and Ernst Chain adapted his work almost 20 years later during World War II. Since then, it has saved millions of lives.

■ Dr. Hans von Ohain of Germany and Sir Frank Whittle of the UK are both considered the inventors of the jet engine. Dr. von Ohain's engine powered a jet that first flew in 1939, followed by Sir Whittle's in 1941.

A child soldier

Sometimes children are forced to fight.
Here is the disturbing story of one such child.
He is 12 years old and lives in Liberia.

They came and took us at night—all the children in our village. One boy tried to escape, but he was caught. His hands were tied, and then they made the rest of us kill him with a stick. I felt sick. I knew this boy from before. At first I refused to kill him, and then they told me they would shoot me.

They pointed a gun at me, so I had to do it. The boy was asking me, "Why are you doing this?" I said I had no choice. I still dream about the boy from my village who I killed. I see him in my dreams when he talks to me and says that I killed him for nothing, and I am crying.

Child soldiers in Liberia. In some conflicts, children are forced to have guns.

Fact bank

■ The United Nations defines a child soldier as being under 18. There are some fighters in war-torn regions of the world who are as young as 8 years old.

■ There were about 100,000 child soldiers in Africa in 2004.

■ Most child soldiers are recruited by armed groups and not by regular government supported forces.

Child soldiers in Myanmar (Burma).

My job was to run out into the battleground and grab weapons, watches, wallets, and any ammunition from the dead soldiers and bring it all back. This was difficult. The enemy could see you and try to shoot you as you ran out and back again. I was given this job because I was the smallest. Sometimes when I fell asleep on sentry duty, I was beaten by my corporal. He beat me like a dog, like I was an animal and not a human being.

I could not run away. If they caught me, they would kill me. And where would I go? At least if I stayed with my commander he would feed me, and I would have somewhere to sleep.

Ask yourself this . . .

■ Why do you think children in some parts of the world are recruited to fight at such a young age?

■ How old are you? If you were forced to kill your neighbor, how do you think you might be affected?

■ Being part of an armed group gave this child access to food and shelter that he may not otherwise have had. Do you think it's worth the risks he took? What else could he have done?

An atomic bomb survivor

The atomic bomb is the most devastating of all weapons. There are enough bombs in existence to destroy Earth many times over. The only two that have ever been used during a war were dropped by the U.S. on Japan in August 1945. Sakue Shimohira witnessed the horrific effects.

My name is Sakue Shimohira. I was 10 when the atomic bomb fell on my town, Nagasaki. When the air-raid siren sounded, I fled with my sister to the nearby shelter. My mom stayed behind to draw some water from the well. After a while, the alarm was lifted and everyone got ready to leave. Then there was a sudden brilliant flash of light, and I passed out. When I opened my eyes, I couldn't believe what I saw. Some people were so horribly burned that it was impossible to tell if they were men or women.

We began to cry hysterically. Luckily my father found us and led us out of the shelter. The ground was littered with the dead and dying and the air was thick with the stench of burning. When we got home, we found my mom's body. The whole thing fills me with enormous rage and sorrow.

Atomic bombs keep killing long after they have exploded. Thousands of people who survived the blast died through radiation sickness, and for years, many more suffered from illnesses caused by that terrible weapon. Even today, 60 years later, people suffer.

Sakue Shimohira survived the bombing.

Fact bank

■ Many people believe that after World War II, a nuclear conflict between the U.S. and the Soviet Union was prevented because there was a "balance of power" of weapons on both sides. Today, there are still over 20,000 nuclear warheads worldwide. Each nuclear warhead is up to 10 times more powerful than the bomb that fell on Nagasaki.

■ Since 1947, the Doomsday Clock has been a symbol of how close the world is to nuclear disaster. It currently stands at 7 minutes to midnight— midnight is nuclear war. In 1953, it stood at 2 minutes to midnight.

A military parade in North Korea. North Korea is one of several countries thought to be developing nuclear weapons.

Ask yourself this . . .

■ Do you think nuclear weapons act as a deterrent? What would happen if every country had them?

■ Is it right to wage war against another country if it is believed they are developing nuclear weapons, or would it only cause more problems?

■ What do you think Sakue Shimohira would say about the development of more nuclear weapons?

A pacifist

Pacifists believe that war is never right. Bradford Lyttle is 77 years old, and he has spent his life campaigning against armed conflict.

I believe that all conflict can and should be resolved through non-violent means and that any violence, anytime, anywhere, is wrong.

Don't misunderstand me—I know that there have been many tyrants throughout history who have committed horrible crimes, but I sincerely believe that armed self-defense is not the best way to oppose evil. In fact, the belief that you win by being capable of killing more people and destroying more property than your enemy is evil itself.

Fact bank

■ Pacifists believe that all violence is wrong, even in self-defense. Bradford Lyttle has led protests about many wars. He has even run for office in the U.S. presidential election to publicize his views, which were inspired by the Indian leader Mahatma Gandhi.

■ Gandhi and his followers resisted British rule of India through acts of non-violent, civil disobedience, such as refusing to obey laws or pay taxes.

Bradford Lyttle is opposed to violence.

Furthermore, as a pacifist I think that the very existence of chemical, biological, and nuclear weapons is a danger to the world and [these weapons] have to be dismantled as quickly as possible. The longer they are here, the more chance there is of a devastating accident. And think of the money that's being spent! What a better place the world would be if the money was redirected into improving people's lives rather than ending them.

Peace parade in Rome, Italy. Many people believe that a peaceful solution can be found to most problems.

Ask yourself this . . .

■ Is being a pacifist just a nice idea, rather than a realistic way of living? When do you think it wouldn't work?

■ Could you stand by and do nothing if someone you love was being harmed? How far do you think you would go?

■ Both Bradford Lyttle and Major Tom Fisher would say they were "working for peace"—who is right?

Terrorism

On October 12, 2002, a bomb destroyed a nightclub in Bali, Indonesia. The testimonies below are from Amrozi bin Nurhasyim, who was sentenced to death for helping to plant the bomb, and from Erik De Haart, who was outside the club where six of his friends were killed.

The bomber

I bought the chemicals for the bomb and the van that held it. I have a pride in my heart for what happened. I am sorry for the deaths of the Balinese people, but for the white people—it serves them right, especially the Americans. But it was the only way to drive foreigners out of Indonesia. They were destroying our morals. Muslim people were deserting their places of worship and turning to places of sin, like nightclubs. Let them kill me. I am happy to die a martyr. After me, there will be a million more Amrozis.

Amrozi bin Nurhasyim in court.

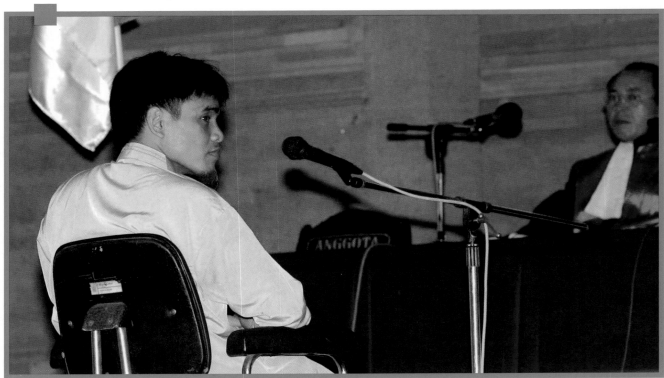

Fact bank

■ More than 200 citizens from 21 countries died in the Bali bombing, including 88 Australians, 38 Indonesians, 23 Britons, and 7 Americans.

Some of the victims of the Bali bombing.

■ The effect of terrorism is to spread fear and terror across a much wider area than just the scene of the act.

■ People who accept the terrorists' explanation for their actions consider them to be freedom fighters and, if they die, call them martyrs. Many Muslims are opposed to the use of violence.

A casualty

The best thing I can do is show those responsible that they haven't changed my life and I still live on my terms. But I really didn't want the death sentence to be given to Amrozi bin Nurhasyim. I'd like him to be tucked in a nice, deep, dark jail somewhere and held there for the rest of his life, to suffer in the same way that all those people who lost children have suffered. But I'll never achieve closure. It will never go away. Each night, I still think about the bodies and the burned people.

Ask yourself this . . .

■ Do you think Amrozi bin Nurhasyim should have been sentenced to death? Why?

■ Sometimes hostages are taken by terrorists and their lives are threatened if certain demands are not met. In such circumstances, should governments ever negotiate with terrorists? Why?

Classroom conflict

Bullying exists in some form in all schools, but teachers can only do something about it if they know it's happening. As this teacher says, it's not easy to find out the facts.

It's good to tell kids to report things as soon as they happen, but in my experience bullies usually wait until they are away from the glare of teachers to make their move. Recess is often the crisis-point. By the time we hear about it, the bully has had time to come up with a plausible lie to cover his or her actions. It is so hard to know who's telling the truth. There are always two sides to an argument.

It's better for victims of bullying to talk about it.

Often, I find that bullies have been victims themselves. They may have suffered in silence for ages, bottled up their anger, and taken it out on someone "weaker." It's a vicious cycle that needs to be broken.

In an assembly last week, the principal spoke about the new signs in the corridor that say, "Being bullied? Speak up—don't take the law into your own hands!" We are also trying a "playground buddy" program, where a few of the older children will be trained as counselors and will wear special hats during recess so that a bullied child can go to them and feel safe.

Bullying can take many forms, but physical violence is often the worst.

Fact bank

Bullying is a form of conflict and can take many forms:

■ Verbal—where a bully insults or abuses their victim.

■ Physical—where a bully hits, kicks, or steals from their victim.

■ Indirect—where a bully spreads rumors about their victim.

■ Direct but anonymous—by text messaging and E-mail.

Ask yourself this . . .

■ Why do you think victims of physical bullying are encouraged not to hit back?

■ What are the most effective ways to "stand up" to a bully?

■ Look back through the book— what advice might the people we have met on these pages give to a bully and their victim?

What do war and conflict have to do with me?

You may have experienced war and conflict only in the movies or in pretend playground battles. Maybe the biggest conflict in your life is over the TV remote control. Perhaps you're being bullied at home or in school. Most individuals don't have direct experience with war but, like the people quoted on these two pages, they still have opinions about it. To find out more about them look at the Web sites. They will also help you answer the following questions. Use all of this information to form your own opinion about war and conflict.

How easy would it be to live as a non-violent pacifist?

"The chain reaction of evil—hate begetting hate, wars producing more wars—must be broken, or we shall be plunged into the dark abyss of annihilation."
　　—Dr. Martin Luther King, Jr., Civil Rights activist and winner of the Nobel Peace Prize

"There are no warlike people, just warlike leaders."
　　—Ralph Bunche, winner of the Nobel Peace Prize

■ www.uspacifistparty.org
■ www.nobelprize.org/nobel_prizes/peace/

What's the difference between Major Tom Fisher and a suicide bomber—after all, they are both willing to die for what they believe in?

"One day we must come to see that peace is not merely a distant goal we seek, but that it is a means by which we arrive at that goal. We must pursue peaceful ends through peaceful means."

> —Dr. Martin Luther King, Jr., Civil Rights activist and winner of the Nobel Peace Prize

"It isn't poverty that breeds terrorism, but terrorism that breeds poverty."

> —Dan Gillerman, United Nations (UN) official

■ www.thekingcenter.org
■ www.dhs.gov

In wars, people kill each other —can that ever be right?

"So long as there are men, there will be wars."

> – Albert Einstein, scientist and winner of the Nobel Prize (1879–1955)

"The purpose of all war is ultimately peace."

> – Saint Augustine, Christian leader (354–430 A.D.)

■ www.albert-einstein.org
■ www.catholic-forum.com/saints/sainta02.htm

Is a country that fights with a weaker country behaving like a playground bully?

"Looking for peace is like looking for a turtle with a mustache: You won't be able to find it."

> —Ajahn Chah, Buddhist monk

"If the battle for civilization comes down to the wimps versus the barbarians, the barbarians are going to win."

> —Thomas Sowell, lecturer and author

■ www.forestsangha.org/aboutchah.htm
■ www.tsowell.com

Web sites

The Web sites below feature more information, news articles, and stories that you can use to help form your own opinions. Use the information carefully and consider its source before drawing any conclusions.

www.un.org/peace
The "peace and security" section of the United Nations' Web site featuring up-to-date information on current crises, peacekeeping missions, and international programs.

www.antiwar.com
Political news-based Web site of the Randolph Bourne Institute, featuring a wide range of up-to-date articles from countries worldwide.

www.amnesty.org
Web site of Amnesty International (AI), the worldwide campaign for internationally recognized human rights that features reports and the latest human rights news from around the world.

www.usmc.mil
Official Web site of the United States Marine Corps. Read more stories from active Marines and find out about current operations.

www.stopbullyingnow. hrsa.gov
Web site sponsored by the U.S. Department of Health and Human Services that features cartoons, games, and helpful information about bullying for students and adults.

www.cnn.com
Current news stories from CNN, including breaking news about war and conflict throughout the world.

Glossary

Air-raid siren – loud alarm to warn people of an attack.

Ammunition – bombs and bullets fired by weapons.

Atomic bomb – a bomb that has great explosive power.

Biological weapons – weapons that spread disease.

Civilian – someone who is not a soldier.

Comrade – a close friend.

Counselor – a person who listens to people's problems and gives helpful advice.

Deserter – a soldier who abandons his or her duty.

Deterrent – something designed to discourage an enemy from attacking.

Dismantle – to take apart.

Doomsday Clock – a picture clock that shows how close the world is to nuclear war.

Enlisting – joining.

Hostage – someone held captive against his or her will.

Marine – an American soldier who serves at sea, on land, and in the air.

Martyrs – people who are willing to sacrifice their lives for what they believe in.

Nuclear weapon – see entry for atomic bomb.

Sentry duty – when a soldier stands guard.

Surrender – to stop fighting.

United Nations – an organization that promotes peace and security.

Veteran – someone who has served in the armed forces.

Victim – a person who is harmed by someone else.

http://hrw.org/campaigns /crp/index.htm
Web site of the Human Rights Watch (HRW) that contains true stories of the experiences of children throughout the world; HRW is dedicated to the protection of human rights worldwide.

www.oxfam.org/eng
Web site of Oxfam International, an organization that works with partners to find solutions to poverty, suffering, and injustice.

Index